Open Closed Open

Other Books by Yehuda Amichai

Poems

Songs of Jerusalem and Myself

Amen

Time

Love Poems

Great Tranquillity: Questions and Answers

Travels: A Bilingual Edition

Poems of Jerusalem

Even a Fist Was Once an Open Palm with Fingers

The Selected Poetry of Yehuda Amichai

Yehuda Amichai: A Life of Poetry 1948–1994

Yehuda Amichai

Open Closed Open

POEMS

Translated from the Hebrew by
Chana Bloch and Chana Kronfeld

Harcourt, Inc.
NEW YORK   SAN DIEGO   LONDON

For my wife, Hana,
and for my children,
Ron, David, and Emmanuella

Compilation copyright © 2000 by Yehuda Amichai
Copyright © 2000 by Chana Bloch and Chana Kronfeld

Originally published in Hebrew as *Patuach Sagur Patuach.*

Library of Congress Cataloging-in-Publication Data available on request.

Designed by Lori McThomas Buley
Text set in Centaur MT
Printed in the United States of America
First edition
A B C D E F G H I J

CONTENTS

The Amen Stone   1

I Wasn't One of the Six Million:
And What Is My Life Span? Open Closed Open   3

I Foretell the Days of Yore   9

The Bible and You, the Bible and You, and Other Midrashim   17

Once I Wrote *Now and in Other Days:*
Thus Glory Passes, Thus Pass the Psalms   29

Gods Change, Prayers Are Here to Stay   37

David, King of Israel, Is Alive: Thou Art the Man   49

My Parents' Lodging Place   55

What Has Always Been   61

Israeli Travel: Otherness Is All, Otherness Is Love   67

Evening Promenade on Valley of the Ghosts Street   75

Summer and the Far End of Prophecy   81

Houses (Plural); Love (Singular)   87

The Language of Love and Tea with Roasted Almonds   91

The Precision of Pain and the Blurriness of Joy:
The Touch of Longing Is Everywhere   99

In My Life, on My Life   107

Jewish Travel: Change Is God and Death Is His Prophet   115

Names, Names, in Other Days and in Our Time   125

Jerusalem, Jerusalem, Why Jerusalem?   133

Conferences, Conferences: Malignant Words, Benign Speech   145

My Son Was Drafted   153

Autumn, Love, Commercials   161

And Who Will Remember the Rememberers?   167

The Jewish Time Bomb   173

Notes   174

Acknowledgments   183

Open Closed Open

The Amen Stone

On my desk there is a stone with the word "Amen" on it,
a triangular fragment of stone from a Jewish graveyard destroyed
many generations ago. The other fragments, hundreds upon hundreds,
were scattered helter-skelter, and a great yearning,
a longing without end, fills them all:
first name in search of family name, date of death seeks
dead man's birthplace, son's name wishes to locate
name of father, date of birth seeks reunion with soul
that wishes to rest in peace. And until they have found
one another, they will not find perfect rest.
Only this stone lies calmly on my desk and says "Amen."
But now the fragments are gathered up in lovingkindness
by a sad good man. He cleanses them of every blemish,
photographs them one by one, arranges them on the floor
in the great hall, makes each gravestone whole again,
one again: fragment to fragment,
like the resurrection of the dead, a mosaic,
a jigsaw puzzle. Child's play.

I Wasn't One of the Six Million:
And What Is My Life Span?
Open Closed Open

1

My life is the gardener of my body. The brain—a hothouse closed tight
with its flowers and plants, alien and odd
in their sensitivity, their terror of becoming extinct.
The face—a formal French garden of symmetrical contours
and circular paths of marble with statues and places to rest,
places to touch and smell, to look out from, to lose yourself
in a green maze, and Keep Off and Don't Pick the Flowers.
The upper body above the navel—an English park
pretending to be free, no angles, no paving stones, naturelike,
humanlike, in our image, after our likeness,
its arms linking up with the big night all around.
And my lower body, beneath the navel—sometimes a nature preserve,
wild, frightening, amazing, an unpreserved preserve,
and sometimes a Japanese garden, concentrated, full of
forethought. And the penis and testes are smooth
polished stones with dark vegetation between them,
precise paths fraught with meaning
and calm reflection. And the teachings of my father
and the commandments of my mother
are birds of chirp and song. And the woman I love
is seasons and changing weather, and the children at play
are my children. And the life my life.

2

I've never been in those places where I've never been
and never will be, I have no share in the infinity of light-years and
    dark-years,
but the darkness is mine, and the light, and my time
is my own. The sand on the seashore—those infinite grains
are the same sand where I made love in Achziv and Caesarea.

The years of my life I have broken into hours, and the hours into
    minutes
and seconds and fractions of seconds. These, only these,
are the stars above me
that cannot be numbered.

3

And what is my life span? I'm like a man gone out of Egypt:
the Red Sea parts, I cross on dry land,
two walls of water, on my right hand and on my left.
Pharaoh's army and his horsemen behind me. Before me the desert,
perhaps the Promised Land, too. That is my life span.

4

Open closed open. Before we are born, everything is open
in the universe without us. For as long as we live, everything is closed
within us. And when we die, everything is open again.
Open closed open. That's all we are.

5

What then is my life span? Like shooting a self-portrait.
I set up the camera a few feet away on something stable
(the one thing that's stable in this world),
I decide on a good place to stand, near a tree,
run back to the camera, press the timer,
run back again to that place near the tree,
and I hear the ticking of time, the whirring
like a distant prayer, the click of the shutter like an execution.
That is my life span. God develops the picture
in His big darkroom. And here is the picture:
white hair on my head, eyes tired and heavy,
eyebrows black, like the charred lintels

above the windows in a house that burned down.
My life span is over.

6

I wasn't one of the six million who died in the Shoah,
I wasn't even among the survivors.
And I wasn't one of the six hundred thousand who went out of Egypt.
I came to the Promised Land by sea.
No, I was not in that number, though I still have the fire and the smoke
within me, pillars of fire and pillars of smoke that guide me
by night and by day. I still have inside me the mad search
for emergency exits, for soft places, for the nakedness
of the land, for the escape into weakness and hope,
I still have within me the lust to search for living water
with quiet talk to the rock or with frenzied blows.
Afterwards, silence: no questions, no answers.
Jewish history and world history
grind me between them like two grindstones, sometimes
to a powder. And the solar year and the lunar year
get ahead of each other or fall behind,
leaping, they set my life in perpetual motion.
Sometimes I fall into the gap between them to hide,
or to sink all the way down.

7

I believe with perfect faith that at this very moment
millions of human beings are standing at crossroads
and intersections, in jungles and deserts,
showing each other where to turn, what the right way is,
which direction. They explain exactly where to go,
what is the quickest way to get there, when to stop
and ask again. There, over there. The second

turnoff, not the first, and from there left or right,
near the white house, by the oak tree.
They explain with excited voices, with a wave of the hand
and a nod of the head: There, over there, not *that* there, the *other* there,
as in some ancient rite. This too is a new religion.
I believe with perfect faith that at this very moment.

I Foretell the Days of Yore

1

The flight attendants of the next millennium came to me and said:
You can still get a seat on the third millennium before liftoff.
Come with us, dead or alive, we'll take you along. We have no malice,
no defenses, but we're strong and mobile as constellations;
our eyes are closed but we can see.
We are women who glide between life and death.
You with your seat belts and gear belts and buckles that click shut,
you, sir, you with the noise of a door closing,
we with our voices of glide and whisper.
Our belts are not for safety or for holding up our clothes,
they are snakes, they are decoration. Gliding spirals,
we are acrobats looping the loops of wish and would.
You with your warm worries and emotions
heavy as cow dung in the field,
you with the sweat of your death like an afterlife perfume.

2

We are the flight attendants of the next millennium, buoyant brides
with no excess baggage of bridegrooms,
while you are weighed down by the stripes and checks on your clothing.
You with the flicking colors of traffic lights, permitted, forbidden—
for us color changes are fluid. You with your strict demarcations
of sacred and profane, outerwear and underwear; for us
everything is like water within water. You with your little excitements
and attachments, your oaths and your vows,
your buttons and snaps, your comb and your qualms,
hairbrush and despairs, you with your loneliness
and the compassion of wombs, of testicles and stiff members.
For us everything is smooth and transparent—pliable glass.
You with your conjunctions and prepositions,
you with your spirit, your respiration and resuscitation,

your distance and intimacy. We are the world to come,
come with us, we'll preserve you like a potsherd, like a symbol,
like a lion of stone, and in the year 2024
we will celebrate your hundredth birthday.

3

I am a prophet of what has already been. I read the past in the palm
of the woman I love, I forecast the winter rains that have fallen,
I am an expert on the snows of yesteryear, I conjure the spirits
of what has always been, I foretell the days of yore,
I draw up the blueprints for a house right after it's torn down,
I prophesy the small room with its few pieces of furniture—
a towel draped over the only chair to dry,
the arch of the high window, curved like our bodies in love.

4

I am a prophet of the past. And how do you see and foresee
the future? As when a man sees a woman with a beautiful body
walking before him in the street
and looks at her with desire, but she doesn't turn
to look back, just smooths her skirt a little,
pulls her blouse tight, fixes the back of her hair, then
without turning toward the man's gaze
quickens her step. That's
what the future is like.

5

Life, I think, is hard work:
As Jacob labored to be with Rachel seven years
plus seven plus seven times seven, I've worked
to be one with my life, like the beloved Rachel
and to be one with my death, like the beloved Rachel.

6

Straight from the fear of loss I plunged into the fear of being lost.
I couldn't stay long enough between them
in the sweet little no man's land of my everlasting
passing days. My hands are the hands of search and test,
hands of hope, hands of gloom,
always fumbling among papers on tables
or in drawers, in closets and in my clothes
which have seen their share of loss.
With hands that search for what is already lost, I caress your face,
and with hands afraid of loss I hold you close
and like a blind man feel my way around your eyes, your mouth,
wandering, wondering, wandering, wondering.
Because hands afraid of loss are the only hands for love.

Once I saw a violinist playing and I thought: Between
his right hand and his left—only the violin,
but what a between, what music!

7

Between the eve of the holiday and the final day
the holiday itself gets squeezed, between
longing for the past and longing for the future
the spirit is ground up as if by two heavy grindstones,
upper and lower. Between "In the East is my heart" and "I dwell
at the end of the West," the sea goes dry. Between the preventive
lament of before and the lament of after, joy shuts down.
Between hanging out flags for the holiday and folding them up again,
the wind blows and sweeps everything away.
The song of the turtledove mourning is the song
of the turtledove wooing. With the same body
that stoops to pick up a fallen something from the floor,
I bow down to God. That is my faith, my religion.

8

Counting, counting, I hear them counting
as if out for the count at the end of the fight. When I was born
they counted to ten and they went on counting.
Now the referees and the crowd have gone home,
the lights in the arena are off, I got up long ago and headed
for my life, and they are still counting.
The pleasant evening breeze is only the towel
the trainer waves in my face, believing
I'll keep up the fight. Counting, counting I hear,
sometimes out loud, sometimes in a whisper
or in a woman's voice making love, sometimes counting
like taking inventory, taking a blood count or a pulse.
Sometimes a countdown or a count-up into the future,
in a solo voice or in unison, like a Greek chorus.
And they go on counting, deciphering ciphers before
my death and after it, counting
the spheres of the stars and the uppermost spheres,
those heights so high
the singing can have no end.

9

At times I think life is like a terrible accident,
a car rolling off the road down into the abyss, slow or fast.
I roll and reconcile,
reconcile and roll.

10

Life, I think, is a series of rehearsals
for the real show. In a rehearsal you can still
make changes, cut out a sentence, add a line of dialogue, switch
actors, directors, theaters—up until the real show.
Then there is no changing. And it makes no difference

that you can't make a difference:
The show closes right after opening night.

11

All the motions and the positions in my body—
it's already been done.
I sit on a chair and think like Rodin's Thinker.
Ever since I sat folded up in my mother's belly,
I have carried inside me the wisdom of the folding chair.
My arms are raised like Moses' arms when he raised the Tablets of
    the Law,
my arms are raised without holding a thing,
a bit in disbelief, a bit in despair.
I give hugs like King David on the roof, or helpless hugs
like Jesus on the cross, but the palms of my hands
are free, I am free, though everything
has already come to pass. I have learned to swim
in the stream of consciousness, and I know a thing or two
about the difference between wire and wireless, God and
No-God, jet and chopper, a door
that opens and closes with a slam
and a revolving door that keeps revolving.

12

Now after many years of living I begin to see
that I rebelled only a little, and I do observe
all the laws and commandments.
I observe the law of gravity, that is, the law of the earth's attraction,
with all my body and with all my might and with all my love;
I observe the law of equilibrium and the law of the conservation
    of matter:
my body and my body, my soul and my soul, my body and my soul.
I abhor a vacuum in my pain and in my joy

I follow the law of water seeking its own level; past and future
are recycled back to me. I rise and I raise with the law of the lever.
I begin to understand, as I would with an old car,
what makes it work, the action of pistons and brakes,
reward and punishment, be fruitful and multiply,
forget and remember, bolts and springs,
fast and slow, and the laws of history.
Thus spake the years of my life unto the days of my life,
thus spake my soul unto the parts of my body.
This is a sermon in the synagogue, this is a eulogy
for the dead, this is burial and this
is resurrection. Thus spake the man.

The Bible and You, the Bible and You,
and Other Midrashim

I

How did Gideon choose his army at the Spring of Harod?
He saw them drinking from the spring,
lapping like dogs or kneeling down, and chose.
But my Gideon went on choosing: What is their way with a woman,
in what position do they make love? And how do they weep,
in a bawling voice or with silent tears,
and how do they eat and how do they sleep, on their belly like a baby,
on their side or on their back, and how do they remember their
    childhood?
And he didn't take those who remember and never forget,
and he didn't take those who forget and never remember.
And one said, I drank from the fountain of longing, and another said,
I've been to the enchanted place, and another said, I've never been there,
and another said, I stayed in the dream with the sound of the rolling
    barley cake
and I am still rolling. And my Gideon was left
with no army no battle no glory at the Spring of Harod. And he drank
kneeling down and he drank lapping, and he
drank and remembered and forgot.

2

The Bible and you, the Bible and you.
As the Torah scroll is read aloud each year
from "In the beginning" to "This is the blessing"
and back to the start, so we two roll together
and every year our love gets a new reading.
Torah, Torah, rah rah rah!
Sometimes in one night we go through
what the Torah goes through in an entire year,
and sometimes on a good day
we go on rolling, further and further,

past the Torah, past the death of Moses,
through Kings and Prophets and Writings all the way to
Chronicles, to the Chronicles of Love
and back to Genesis, the creation of light and of the world.
And each day God says: "And it was evening
and it was morning," but He never says
"twilight." Because twilight is for lovers only.

3

The famous French king said, *Après moi, le déluge!*
Noah the Righteous said, Before me, the flood,
and when he left the ark he declared, The flood is behind me.
But I say, I am right in the middle of the flood,
I am the ark and the animals, clean and unclean,
I am two of a kind, male and female,
I am the remembering animals and the forgetting animals,
and I am the seedling of the vine for a good world
though I cannot drink the wine myself.
In the end I'll be a tall Ararat, lonely and dry,
carrying a strange empty ark on my shoulders
with some leftover love inside it, a remnant
of prayer, a bit of hope.

4

Moses saw the face of God just once and then
forgot. He didn't want to see the desert,
not even the Promised Land, only the face of God.
In the fury of his longing he struck the rock,
climbed Mount Sinai and came down again, broke
the Tablets of the Law, made a golden calf, searched through
fire and smoke, but he could remember only
the strong hand of God and His outstretched arm,

not His face. Moses was like a man who tries to recall
the face of someone he loved, but tries in vain.
He composed a police sketch of God's face
and the face of the burning bush and the face of Pharaoh's daughter
leaning over him, a baby in the ark of bulrushes.
He sent that picture to all the tribes of Israel,
up and down the desert, but no one had seen,
no one knew. Only at the end of his life,
on Mount Nebo, did Moses see and die, kissing
the face of God.

   5

Three sons had Abraham, not just two.
Three sons had Abraham: Yishma-El, Yitzhak and Yivkeh.
First came Yishma-El, "God will hear,"
next came Yitzhak, "he will laugh,"
and the last was Yivkeh, "he will cry."
No one has ever heard of Yivkeh, for he was the youngest,
the son that Father loved best,
the son who was offered up on Mount Moriah.
Yishma-El was saved by his mother, Hagar,
Yitzhak was saved by the angel,
but Yivkeh no one saved.
When he was just a little boy, his father
would call him tenderly, Yivkeh,
Yivkeleh, my sweet little Yivkie—
but he sacrificed him all the same.
The Torah says the ram, but it was Yivkeh.
Yishma-El never heard from God again,
Yitzhak never laughed again,
Sarah laughed only once, then laughed no more.
Three sons had Abraham,

Yishma, "will hear," Yitzhak, "will laugh," Yivkeh, "will cry."
Yishma-El, Yitzhak-El, Yivkeh-El,
God will hear, God will laugh, God will cry.

6

A love song in the biblical style. It is written, "He lifted up his voice
    and said,"
and also "He lifted up his voice and wept." And we two go on lifting
our one voice, raising it up high, higher than the words
and the weeping, to say to each other in that chapter and verse: My love.

7

King Saul never learned how to play or to sing
nor was he taught how to be king.
Oh he's got the blues,
he's nothing to lose
but the moody tune
on his gramophone
and David is its name-oh, David is its name,
its name its name its name.
Round and round the record spins,
with a spear for a needle that begins
to pierce the heart
and deaden the hurt
as it deadens the heart.

8

Our father Jacob, on the beaten track,
carries a ladder on his back

like a window washer to the VIPs.
He does God's windows, if you please.

Only the ladder remains of his dream;
the angels finally ran out of steam.

He carries the ladder again every night
back into his dream and out of sight.

At dawn he wrestles a man to the ground.
The man is a woman. They roll round and round,

they roll till they're ravished, till both of them reel,
clutching at chest and crotch and heel,

day after day, by the first morning light,
till Jacob and angel are too weak to fight.

He will climb up that ladder, if ever he dies,
right out of this world and into the skies

until the world vanishes into thin air.
For all that we know, he is still climbing there.

9

Ruth the Moabite knew all about wheat and wheat fields,
about eyes big with love
and golden stubble after the harvest.
And Naomi, who said, I went out full
and the Lord hath brought me home again empty—
she knew all about the physics of the empty and the full,
about her sons who died, about the stifled cry
of a womb emptying like an accordion
which makes music out of the full and the empty.

10

Sometimes I am all alone like King Saul.
I have to play the music for myself, hurl the spear by myself,

23

then dodge the spear. And I am also the wall
in which the spear lodges, trembling.

11
Two lovers lie together like Isaac on the altar
and it feels good. They don't think about the knife
or about the burnt offering—
she thinks about the ram and he about the angel.
Another version: He is the ram and she is the thicket.
He will die and she will go on growing wild.
Another version: The two of them get up and disappear
among the revelers.

12
Anyone who rises early in the morning is on his own.
He gets himself over to the altar, he is Abraham,
he is Isaac, he's the donkey, the fire,
the knife, the angel,
he's the ram, he is God.

13
Here is the true story of Jacob the lover:
Seven plus seven years vanished forever

in pain and more pain, just to win him a life
under one roof with Rachel, his wife.

She's no princess bewitched, and he is no knight;
they're no beauty-and-beast; not a dragon in sight

for Jacob to slay, snicker-snack, like a man.
Just years of hard labor. No God at hand.

No wizard, no giant, no foe to defeat,
just sheep and shorn fields. In the dust and the heat.

"By the sweat of your brow," quoth the Holy Writ.
So deep runs his love. Like a bottomless pit.

14

How do the visions of the prophets see me?
The burning bush sees me as a man extinguished but alive.
And what does Ezekiel's vision of the chariot say about me?
Look, down there is a man who has no wings,
nor the face of a lion, an ox, or an eagle,
and he can walk only in one direction at a time.
He has no radiance about him, no brightness the color of amber,
just a darkness within. That is his soul.
But if we ever fall from our heights and crash to the ground,
he will pick up the scattered pieces,
and all his life, he will keep trying to put us together again,
to restore us, to raise us back up to the skies.

15

I don't imagine that on the night of the exodus from Egypt,
between midnight and dawn, any couple could lie together
in love. (We could have.) In haste,
blood dripping from lintels and doorposts,
silver and gold dishes clanging in the dark, between the firstborn's
stifled death cry and the shrieking of mothers' wombs
emptying like wineskins. And standing over them, legs wide apart,
the Angel of Death, crotch gaping male and female
like a bloody sun in the thick of frizzled black death.
Sandaled feet slapping against the soft dough of matza
and the flesh of belly and thigh, hard belts
cinched tight at the waist, buckles
scraping against skin, tangled in one another.
To roll like that, locked in eternal love,

with all the rabble from the house of slavery
into the Promised Desert.

16

Waiting rooms. The waiting room of Job
where he waits for the bad news
and his friends sit and talk to him in whispers.
The waiting room of Moses in the desert
where he paces back and forth and doesn't sit still for an instant.
The waiting room of Isaac bound on Mount Moriah, waiting
to go under the knife. The waiting room of Sarah
in the tent before the birth of her son,
and the waiting room of King David up on the roof.
He was waiting for Bathsheba to get out of her bath,
then he sat and waited for Nathan the prophet
to come and curse him. And all of us
wait with them in a rustle of wings
and a flutter of newspapers
and coughs and sighs and whispered conversations—
wait for the door to be opened by the white angel
and behind him the blinding white light.

17

Balaam, Balaam, whose curse turned to blessing and his blessing to love.
Lay sleepless all night and at dawn he dashed off to the hills
to survey the tribes of Israel and deliver his oracle.
But the children of Israel had departed in haste during the night,
light on their feet, free of blessing and curse, and all Balaam could see
was the abandoned camp, tent pegs, bits of rope and campfire embers,
the smell of sheep, the memory of women's perfume, veils
left behind, a dress ripped by hard thistles, broken clay jars,
a bright-colored ribbon and a jackal scrabbling in the garbage, howling.
And Balaam went home, as a man returns to his lover's room

the morning after and finds the room empty, only a crumpled letter,
a white stocking, a comb with hair in it—that is how Balaam longed for
the children of Israel. That Balaam with his oration, man without
    a nation,
whose curse turned to blessing and blessing to love
and love to longing and longing to a pain that has no end.
From his window he could still see the pillar of fire
and the pillar of smoke on the horizon,
and the two shall never meet.

    18

The singer of the Song of Songs sought his beloved so long and hard
that he lost his mind and went looking for her with a simile map
and fell in love with the images he himself had imagined.
He went down to Egypt, for he had written "to a mare among
    Pharaoh's chariots
I compare thee," and he went up to Gilead to see her flowing hair,
for he had written "Thy hair is like a flock of goats flowing down
Mount Gilead," and he went up to the Tower of David, for it says
"Like the Tower of David is thy neck," and he got as far as Lebanon
    and found
no peace, for it says "Thy nose is like the Tower of Lebanon that looks
out toward Damascus," and he wept by the waterfalls
of Ein Gedi, for he had written "Many waters cannot extinguish
this love," and he went looking for doves in Bet Guvrin
and got all the way to Venice, for he had written "My dove in the clefts
    of the rock."
And he dashed off to the desert, for it says "Who is that rising
from the desert like pillars of smoke." And the Bedouin thought
he was one of the crazy prophets, and he thought
he was King Solomon. And he is still wandering, a fugitive and
    a vagabond
with the mark of Love on his forehead. And sometimes he happens upon

the loves of other couples in other times; he even got as far as our home
with its broken roof on the border between Jerusalem
and Jerusalem. And we never even saw him because we
were in each other's arms. He is still wandering, shouting
"You are beautiful, my bride," as if from within a deep sack
of oblivion. And whoever wrote "Love is as fierce as death"—
he understood his own simile only at the end,
understood and loved and died.

Once I Wrote *Now and in Other Days:*
Thus Glory Passes, Thus Pass the Psalms

1

Once I wrote *Now and in Other Days.*
Now I have arrived at those other days.
When I wrote it, they were at the end of the century;
now they are in the past, in the middle of the century.
But the Now is always with me, wherever I go is the Now,
as in the solar system, past and future and I—
always turning, returning. The Now is the sun,
the Now is eternity. Change is God.
And those other days turned into Otherness. On my desk
is a stone with "Amen" written on it, a fragment of a tombstone
from a Jewish grave destroyed a thousand years ago. On my desk
is a piece of torn shrapnel from an exploded grenade.
My children found it at Tel Gath among the spring flowers.
That twisted shrapnel is the angel that redeems me,
the angel that didn't kill me in battle, in those other days.
Perhaps it killed some other person.
Otherness is God. Otherness killed Him. The truth is,
Otherness killed Ruth.

2

When I was young I believed with all my heart
the Huleh swamp had to be drained.
Then all the bright-colored birds fled for their lives.
Now half a century later they are filling it with water again
because it was all a mistake. Perhaps my entire life
I've been living a mistake.
And the God of my childhood, He too
is a mistake, though He is still called God.
But the perfect mistake makes a perfect life,
like perfect faith. The saying "Mistakes happen"
I've turned into a comforting song, and the verse

"All men are false" I've made into a dance tune by day,
a lullaby at night. Amen.

   3
And to this day, I still believe sometimes
the way I used to. When we sang "This is the last battle," I believed,
and when they told me, "This is the last supper" I believed. Since then
my life has filled with last battles and last suppers, like the last wish
of a death-row inmate. And when they say Rosh Hashana,
which means "the Head of the Year," I remember
only the head sometimes, not the hand or the swift foot of Time
passing. And the measure of justice and the measure of mercy were like
getting measured for shoes—to this day I buy shoes a size too big
so they won't pinch my feet. I have learned why this night differs
from all other nights and how it came to be different. And I have
      learned
who ate my porridge and who's been sleeping in my bed.
They told me "I'll be back" and I am still
waiting, and they told me "I'll never come back"
and I am still waiting. And when they told me "Don't ask,"
I began to ask, and I have not stopped asking since.

   4
Oh, the small interrogatives of my life,
hopping, chirping, flitting about,
eluding me since my childhood.
Tiny as birds, light as grasshoppers.
But when I grew up, I made them into heavy affirmatives
like fattened ducks or chickens that come home to roost
and can't rise up and fly:
Whatness, Whyness, Whoness. And birds even heavier than those:
Whereness, Awareness, Whither and Die.

5

Blood turns black when it congeals, grass turns gray and brown when
    it dies.
During a heat wave you have to drink lots of water, in a stone wall
you've got to make little gun slits. All this only
to go on living, to postpone a bit
the hour of death. The way a child leaves
a half-eaten chocolate bar in his pants pocket, to have some
when the other kids have finished all of theirs.

6

As clay jars that sank to the bottom of the sea in ancient times
and are raised from the deep all covered with seaweed,
barnacles and algae, though the shape of the jars remains as it was—
so too the story of my life: the tears are still my tears
and the laughter my laughter. Don't try
to scrub them clean. The laughter is heavy and out of the depths,
and the tears are wreathed in dense beautiful layers from the abyss.
That too is change, that too is another place,
and the ships? They are all up in heaven.

7

Now the Memorial Days have passed. The gap between the names
of streets and the people who live on them is growing
and hope gets more distant from those who are hoping.
Ah, those were the days! The flowering squill in the fall
had the fragrance of yeast cake, and the children
had biblical names. Seasons had the look of orange groves
and people were like trees in the Garden of Eden,
knowledge trees, knowing good and evil.
A new generation wields the hope of the one that is gone
like case-hardened tools to crack open the future,

the disappointments of one generation shore up
the latest in longings and illusions,
a creek is still called a creek even when it's dry
and joy still goes by the name of joy.

8

I want to live till even the words in my mouth are nothing
but vowels and consonants, maybe just vowels, soft sounds.
The soul inside me is the last foreign language I'm learning.
I want to live until all the numbers are sacred,
not just one not just seven not just twelve not just three
but all the numbers, the twenty-three fallen in the battle of Huleikat,
seventeen kilometers to the enchanted place, thirty-four nights,
one hundred twenty-nine days of grace, three hundred thousand
speed-of-light years, forty-three moments of happiness
(and the number of the years of my life still X). The history
of four thousand years in forty-five minutes of a final at school.
And the days and the nights are without number—but
they too shall be numbered—
even infinity will be sacred, and then
I will find perfect rest.

9

Thus glory passes. Thus they pass, the psalms,
crying singing cursing blessing—verses
from the mouths of worshipers: Happy is the man,
Like a tree planted, Happy are they that dwell
in Thy house, All men are false, Servants of the Lord,
My Rock and Redeemer, David and the sons of Korah, hallelujahs,
green pastures, still waters, dark valleys of death.
Thus they pass, like a parade when the circus comes to town
but won't stop, won't open the big tent, elephants
and other animals, the *mea culpa* band

drumming their chests, the we-have-sinned tumblers
and the we-have-betrayed dancers, tightrope walkers, acrobats
hopping Holy, Holy, Holy
with sobs and laughter, bitter cries and sweet song.
Thus it all passes—what was, and what never has been.
Thus the children parade on Arbor Day
with seedlings they won't ever plant,
thus they pass, thus glory passes.

10

Thus glory passes, like a long train without
beginning or end, without cause or purpose. I always
stand to one side at the crossing—the barrier is down—
and I take it all in: carloads of passengers and history, carloads
packed full of war, carloads teeming with human beings
for extermination, windows with the faces of parting
men and women, the high spirits of travelers,
birthdays and deathdays, pleading
and pity and plenty of empty echoing boxcars.
Thus my children pass into their future,
thus the Lord passed over Moses in the Great Desert,
and Moses did not see His face, just cried out,
"Lord, O Lord, merciful and gracious, abundant in goodness
and truth." Thus glory passes. Thus the barrier
is down forever, until the end of my days.

Gods Change, Prayers Are Here to Stay

I

In the street on a summer evening, I saw a woman writing
on a piece of paper spread out against a locked wooden door.
She folded it, tucked it between door and doorpost, and went on her way.
And I didn't see her face, nor the face of the man
who would read what she had written
and I didn't see the words.

On my desk lies a stone with the word "Amen" on it,
a fragment of a tombstone, a remnant from a Jewish graveyard
destroyed a thousand years ago in the town where I was born.
One word, "Amen," carved deep into the stone,
a final hard amen for all that was and never will return,
a soft singing amen, as in prayer:
Amen and amen, may it come to pass.

Tombstones crumble, they say, words tumble, words fade away,
the tongues that spoke them turn to dust,
languages die as people do,
some languages rise again,
gods change up in heaven, gods get replaced,
prayers are here to stay.

2

Jewish theology, Theo, Theo. When I was young I knew a boy
named Theodore, as in Herzl, but his mother called him
home from the playground: Theo, Theo, come home Theo,
don't stay there with the bad boys,
Theo, Theo, lo! Gee.

I don't want an invisible god. I want a god who is seen
but doesn't see, so I can lead him around
and tell him what he doesn't see. And I want

a god who sees and is seen. I want to see
how he covers his eyes, like a child playing blindman's bluff.

I want a god who is like a window I can open
so I'll see the sky even when I'm inside.
I want a god who is like a door that opens out, not in,
but God is like a revolving door, which turns, turns on its hinges
in and out, whirling and turning
without a beginning, without an end.

3

I declare with perfect faith
that prayer preceded God.
Prayer created God,
God created human beings,
human beings create prayers
that create the God that creates human beings.

4

God is a staircase that ascends
to a place that is no longer there, or isn't there yet.
The stairs are my faith, my downfall.
Our father Jacob knew it in his dream.
The angels were just adorning the steps of his ladder
like a fir tree decked out for Christmas,
and the Song of Ascents is a song of praise
to the God of the Stairs.

5

When God packed up and left the country, He left the Torah
with the Jews. They have been looking for Him ever since,
shouting, "Hey, you forgot something, you forgot,"
and other people think shouting is the prayer of the Jews.

Since then, they've been combing the Bible for hints of His whereabouts,
as it says: "Seek ye the Lord while He may be found,
call ye upon Him while He is near." But He is far away.

6

Bird tracks in the sand on the seashore
like the handwriting of someone who jotted down
words, names, numbers and places, so he would remember.
Bird tracks in the sand at night
are still there in the daytime, though I've never seen
the bird that left them. That's the way it is
with God.

7

"Our Father, Our King." What does a father do
when his children are orphans and he
is still alive? What will a father do
when his children have died and he becomes
a bereaved father for all eternity? Cry
and not cry, not forget and not remember.
"Our Father, Our King." What does a king do
in the republic of pain? Give them
bread and circuses like any king,
the bread of memory and the circuses of forgetting,
bread and nostalgia. Nostalgia for God-
and-a-better-world. "Our Father, Our King."

8

The God of the Christians is a Jew, a bit of a whiner,
and the God of the Muslims is an Arab Jew from the desert,
    a bit hoarse.
Only the God of the Jews isn't Jewish.
The way Herod the Edomite was brought in to be king of the Jews,

so God was brought back from the infinite future,
an abstract God: neither painting nor graven image nor tree nor stone.

9

The Jewish people read Torah aloud to God
all year long, a portion a week,
like Scheherazade who told stories to save her life.
By the time Simchat Torah rolls around,
God forgets and they can begin again.

10

Even solitary prayer takes two:
one to sway back and forth
and the one who doesn't move is God.
But when my father prayed, he would stand in his place,
erect, motionless, and force God
to sway like a reed and pray to him.

11

Communal prayer: Is it better to ask "Give us peace"
with cries of woe, or to ask calmly, quietly?
But if we ask calmly, God will think
we don't really need peace and quiet.

12

Morning Psalms. Innocence rises from human beings
like steam from hot food ascending on high, a steam
that turns into God and sometimes into other gods.

13

A collection of ritual objects in the museum: spice boxes
with little flags on top like festive troops
and many fragrant generations of sacrifice,

and the memory of many Sabbath nights that did not end in death.
And happy menorahs and weepy menorahs and oil lamps
with the pouting beaks of chicks like children singing,
their mouths wide open in desire and love.
And long metal hands to point out everything
that is no more. The human hands that held them—
long since underground, severed from the bodies.
Seder plates that rotate at the speed of time
so it seems they are standing still, and kiddush cups
in a row on the shelf like soccer trophies
or victory cups from the track and field of generations.
All is gold of grief, silver of longing,
copper of calamity. A collection of ritual objects
like the gaudy toys of a baby god, the gift
of an aged nation, like the strange instruments
of a ghost orchestra, like some odd motionless
bottom fish deep in the waters of time.
A collection of ritual objects donated by Dr. Feuchtwanger,
Jerusalem dentist. And whoever hears this will assume
a delicate smile on his lips, like well-wrought filigree.

   14
God is like a magician who performs sleight of hand:
causes Himself to appear, makes doves fly out of His pockets,
pulls rabbits out of His sleeve, saws a woman in two,
splits the Red Sea in two, produces ten plagues
and ten commandments with fire and pillars of smoke,
hovers over the waters and vanishes into the wall.
Everyone wants to catch Him in an off moment
and discover how He does it without really doing it.
And everyone wants not to know, not to discover
how He does it, they would like to believe,
each against each. Nothing to nothing.

15

I believe with perfect faith in the resurrection of the dead.
Just as a man who wishes to return to a place he loves
leaves behind a book, a shopping bag, a snapshot, his glasses,
on purpose, so he has to return, that's how the dead leave
the living behind, and they will return.
Once I stood in the mists of a long-ago autumn
in a Jewish cemetery that was abandoned, though not by its dead.
The groundskeeper was an expert on flowers and seasons of the year
but no expert on buried Jews. And he too said: Night after night
they are training for the resurrection of the dead.

16

Whoever put on a tallis when he was young will never forget:
taking it out of the soft velvet bag, opening the folded shawl,
spreading it out, kissing the length of the neckband (embroidered
or trimmed in gold). Then swinging it in a great swoop overhead
like a sky, a wedding canopy, a parachute. And then winding it
around his head as in hide-and-seek, wrapping
his whole body in it, close and slow, snuggling into it like the cocoon
of a butterfly, then opening would-be wings to fly.
And why is the tallis striped and not checkered black-and-white
like a chessboard? Because squares are finite and hopeless.
Stripes come from infinity and to infinity they go
like airport runways where angels land and take off.
Whoever has put on a tallis will never forget.
When he comes out of a swimming pool or the sea,
he wraps himself in a large towel, spreads it out again
over his head, and again snuggles into it close and slow,
still shivering a little, and he laughs and blesses.

17

I'm kosher. I chew my soul-cud
from the enclosed dark of every little thing that happened,
so as not to forget it, not to lose it. Yet again "Renew
our days as of old," yet again adding
one more day to make the holiday last.
If you have ever seen cows in a meadow
chewing their cud, ease and delight on their faces
and a memory of green grass on eye and tongue,
you know what true pleasure is.
I am cleft. I have no hoofs but my soul is
split. That split, that cleft, gives me the strength to stand it all,
and I beat myself up as if beating my breast for my sins
on Rosh Hashana, or like a man looking for something
he has lost, poking in his jacket or his pockets to find it.
Maybe I've forgotten what sin I'm beating my breast for.
To the confession "We have sinned, we have betrayed" I would add
the words "We have forgotten, we have remembered"—two sins
that cannot be atoned for. They ought to cancel each other out
but instead they reinforce one another. Yes, I'm kosher.

18

God's love for His people Israel is an upside-down love.
First crude and physical, with a strong hand and an outstretched arm:
miracles, ten plagues and ten commandments,
almost violent, on a no-name basis.
Then more: more emotion, more soul
but no body, an unrequited ever-longing love
for an invisible god in the high heavens. A hopeless love.

19

We are all children of Abraham
but also the grandchildren of Terah, Abraham's father.
And maybe it's high time the grandchildren
did unto their father as he did unto his
when he shattered his idols and images, his religion, his faith.
That too would be the beginning of a new religion.

20

The sound of a drawer closing—the voice of God,
the sound of a drawer opening—the voice of love,
but it could also be the other way around.
Footsteps approaching—the voice of love,
footsteps retreating—the voice of God
who left the country without notice, temporarily forever.
A book that stays open on the table beside a pair of glasses—
God. A closed book and a lamp that stays lit—
love. A key turning in the door without a sound—
God. A key hesitating—love and hope.
But it could also be the other way around.
A sacrifice of a fragrant scent to God,
a sacrifice of the other senses to love:
a sacrifice of touch and caress, of sight and of sound,
a sacrifice of taste.
But it could also be the other way around.

21

I studied love in my childhood in my childhood synagogue
in the women's section with the help of the women behind the partition
that locked up my mother with all the other women and girls.
But the partition that locked them up locked me up
on the other side. They were free in their love while I remained
locked up with all the men and boys in my love, my longing.

I wanted to be there with them and to know their secrets
and say with them, "Blessed be He who has made me
according to His will." And the partition—
a lace curtain white and soft as summer dresses, swaying
on its rings and loops of wish and would,
lu-lu loops, lullings of love in the locked room.
And the faces of women like the face of the moon behind the clouds
or the full moon when the curtain parts: an enchanted
cosmic order. At night we said the blessing
over the moon outside, and I
thought about the women.

22

I studied love in the synagogue of my childhood,
I sang "Come, O Sabbath bride" on Friday nights
with a bridegroom's fever, I practiced longing for the days of the
    Messiah,
I conducted yearning drills for the days of yore that will not return.
The cantor serenades his love out of the depths,
Kaddish is recited over lovers who remain together,
the male bird dresses up in a blaze of color.
And we dress the rolled-up Torah scrolls in silken petticoats
and gowns of embroidered velvet
held up by narrow shoulder straps.
And we kiss them as they are passed around the synagogue,
stroking them as they pass, as they pass,
as we pass.

23

After Auschwitz, no theology:
From the chimneys of the Vatican, white smoke rises—
a sign the cardinals have chosen themselves a pope.
From the crematoria of Auschwitz, black smoke rises—

a sign the conclave of Gods has not yet chosen
the Chosen People.
After Auschwitz, no theology:
the numbers on the forearms
of the inmates of extermination
are the telephone numbers of God,
numbers that do not answer
and now are disconnected, one by one.

After Auschwitz, a new theology:
the Jews who died in the Shoah
have now come to be like their God,
who has no likeness of a body and has no body.
They have no likeness of a body and they have no body.

David, King of Israel, Is Alive:
Thou Art the Man

1

Lately I've been thinking a lot about King David.
Not the one who is alive forever in the song,
and not the one who is dead forever
under the heavy carpets on his tomb that is not really his tomb,
but the one who played and played for Saul
and kept dodging the spear until he became king.
David changed his tune and pretended to be mad to save
his life; as for me, I change my tune and pretend to be sane
to save my life. If he were alive today
he would tell me: No, it's the other way around.
Every nation had a first king once
like a first love. And the other way around.

2

King David loves Bathsheba,
hugs her tight, fondles her with the same hands
that cut off the head of Goliath,
the very same hands. The same man who rent his clothes
and scattered ashes on his head when his son died,
the very same man. When the sun
rose in the east, he rose up over Bathsheba
like the lion on the banner of Jerusalem
and said to her: Thou art the woman.
And she to him: Thou art the man!
Before long, he would hear the very same words
from the prophet: Thou art the man!

3

King David lies with Bathsheba on the rooftop,
they are heavy as a cloud and light as a cloud.
Her untamed black hair and the wild red hair of his beard
entangled. They have never seen each other's ears

and never will. He acts weak, weepy, lost, betrayed,
escapes into her body and hides inside it
as in the caves and crevices when he fled
from Saul. She counts his battle scars.
You will be mine, she says,
you will be a tower, a citadel, a city, a street, a hotel,
you will be names, names, and in the end
you will be a wadi for two lovers in the desert in 1965:
Nahal David in Ein Gedi.

4

King David took Bathsheba in the hours
between midnight and dawn.
Those are the best hours for a surprise attack
and the best time for making love.
He declared: "Thou art permitted unto me now—
as of this moment you are a widow, the battle is over
in Rabbah." In their bodies, David and Bathsheba
mimicked the death throes
of Uriah the Hittite in battle. Their cries carried
until Yom Kippur and up to our very own day;
the instruments of their love rang out like the bells of Bethlehem
where he was born. He took her from the west
the way his descendants turn east to pray.

5

King David loves many women. He has an ark of love
full of beautiful women, like a holy ark filled with Torah scrolls
brilliant in their beauty, crammed with commands and prohibitions
of Shalt and Shalt Not, weighted with ornaments,
round and sweet as Sephardi Torah scrolls,
heavy as Ashkenazi scrolls with their massive crowns,
dressed in silk and lace and soft velvet embroidered in many colors,

the breastplate hanging like a pendant, and the slender
hand-shaped pointers of silver inlaid with precious stones.
And on Simchat Torah, the Feast of the Law, which is
the Feast of Love, he takes them all out of the ark,
lines them up, kisses them one by one and hugs them,
makes seven rounds and dances with every one,
even with Michal and Merab who never in their lives
wanted him to dance. Then he puts them back
into the depths of the ark, closes the heavy curtain,
and sits down to write the psalms.

6

And all the women said, He loved me best of all,
but Abishag the Shunamite, the girl who came to him in his old age
to keep him warm, she is the only one who said:
I kept him warm, stroked his battle scars and his love scars,
I anointed him with oil, not for kingship but for cure.
I never heard him play or sing, but I wiped his mouth,
his toothless mouth, when I fed him sweet porridge.
I never saw his hands in battle but I kissed
his old white hands.

I am the poor man's ewe lamb, warm and full of compassion,
I came to him from the pasture
as he came from pasture to kingship.
I am the poor man's ewe lamb that rose out of the parable
and I am yours until death comes between us.

My Parents' Lodging Place

I

I passed the cemetery where my parents are buried—
in a poem Ibn Ezra called it "my parents' lodging place."
I didn't go in, just passed by on the road outside the wall.
I wave to my parents whenever I pass, my soul shaped like a hand.
My soul changes shape: sometimes it's my hair in the wind,
sometimes my aching feet as they walk
or my cheerful feet skipping, sometimes my eyes, my eyelids,
sometimes even my eyelashes—all these are my soul.
Peace to my parents, peace to their dust,
peace to their lodging place in Jerusalem.

2

In their great love my parents saved me from disappointment,
from pain and sorrow. Now I am left with their savings
plus the pain I would like to spare my children.
How all those savings have piled up on me!
My parents always told me, "I'll show you,"
sometimes threatening, sometimes in a voice of sweet love:
I'll show you. Just you wait, I'll show you.
"Someday you'll learn," sternly. "Someday you'll learn,"
in a soothing, reassuring voice.
"Do whatever you want," yelling and screaming,
and "Do what you want, you're a free person,"
like the good angels singing in chorus.
You don't know what you want,
you don't know what you want.

3

My mother was a prophet and didn't know it.
Not like Miriam the prophetess dancing with cymbals and tambourines,
not like Deborah who sat under the palm tree and judged the people,
not like Hulda who foretold the future,

but my own private prophet, silent and stubborn.
I am obliged to fulfill everything she said
and I'm running out of lifetime.
My mother was a prophet when she taught me
the do's and don'ts of everyday, paper verses
for one-time use: You'll be sorry,
you'll get exhausted, that will do you good, you'll feel
like a new person, you'll really love it, you
won't be able, you won't like that, you'll never manage
to close it, I knew you wouldn't remember, wouldn't
forget give take rest, yes you can you can.
And when my mother died, all her little predictions came together
in one big prophecy that will last
until the vision of the end of days.

4

My father was God and didn't know it. He gave me
the Ten Commandments not in thunder and not in anger,
not in fire and not in a cloud, but gently
and with love. He added caresses and tender words,
"would you" and "please." And chanted "remember" and "keep"
with the same tune, and pleaded and wept quietly
between one commandment and the next: Thou shalt not
take the name of thy Lord in vain, shalt not take, not in vain,
please don't bear false witness against your neighbor.
And he hugged me tight and whispered in my ear,
Thou shalt not steal, shalt not commit adultery, shalt not kill.
And he lay the palms of his wide-open hands on my head
with the Yom Kippur blessing: Honor, love, that thy days
may be long upon this earth. And the voice of my father—
white as his hair. Then he turned his face to me one last time,
as on the day he died in my arms, and said, I would like to add

two more commandments:
the Eleventh Commandment, "Thou shalt not change,"
and the Twelfth Commandment, "Thou shalt change. You will change."
Thus spoke my father, and he turned and walked away
and disappeared into his strange distances.

What Has Always Been

I

The poet Rachel sang "Perhaps none of this has ever been."
I want to sing of what has always been,
what has truly been,
for what has been is what shall ever be, like the sun,
and the word "perhaps" is the moon that refines everything with its
    gentle light.
I want to sing of Russian shirts embroidered in the colors of love
and the colors of death, Russian shirts buttoned up or open at
    the throat
for easy breathing, for singing and hope.
Russian shirts like monarch butterflies or winged angels.
I want to sing for those who had the voice of Jacob
and the hands of Esau, the color of Jacob's eyes and Esau's smell
    of a field.
In the Valley of Jezreel, in the west, near the foothills of the Carmel,
I know some people. My cousin from the moshav
was a commanding officer there,
my cousin Asher, who with the pistol in his hand
killed the greatest enemy of his life, the cowardly
cancer that hid inside his body and died with him.

2

Now two generations of forgetting have passed
and the first generation of remembering has come. Woe to us
that we have already come to remember
because memories are the hard shell over an empty heart.
Soon people will walk about the fields and cities
and like nature lovers holding a Field Guide to Plants, they will hold
a Field Guide to Human Beings. And they will call out to one another:
Look, I found it, I wasn't mistaken, here are the distinguishing features,
the typical color of eyes and of hair, the characteristic smile, the scent
and the name, this one was a friend, a friend of a friend, that one

a woman from long ago, this one is father-shaped,
that one is me-shaped and you-shaped,
when are you in bloom when do you wither, this is the scientific
name, that's the common name among friends and lovers,
this is a name without a man, and this, a man without a name.
And that's the way it was.

    3
East of the valley, facing Mount Gilboa,
I know that man Nahum who was our commander
in the battles for the distant Negev. The last time I saw him
he was still healthy, his voice quiet, measured, a voice accustomed
to bereavement, to whatever was and will be,
with a wink to Death in his intelligent eyes.
He sat facing me, and behind him Mount Gilboa.
There he sits, his back to the Gilboa. Mountain back
to mountain back. What has always been,
mountain and memory, "remember" and "keep" in one breath.
Decisions taken at night turned into garden flowers
and those not taken, into wildflowers down the mountainside.
But the Gilboa, but Nahum's mountain back.

    4
In the waiting rooms of forgetting
landscapes on the wall turn slowly
into portraits, eyes and nose, forehead and chin,
even as portraits turn into landscapes,
mountain, valley, forest, field.

    5
Evening. Between Gath and Galon, on a day of dust and heat,
a young woman walks in the place where we mustered once
for battle on that terrible hill. Between Gath and Galon, between

the harvest festivals of spring and fall,
in a harvested field. Hay and straw are also hallelujah gifts of God.
Joy cannot speak, joy sings from her mouth.
Her body is all seven species—wheat barley grapevine and fig
pomegranate olive and date, all seven species.
Her shorts are short and her legs long, and her face looks like our hopes
and her eyes are the color of our chances, and the color of sunset is like
the color of her new love. (And when was the last time
she cried?) The way she moves between past and future,
between it-was-good and it-may-yet-be, between doubt and certainty,
sways in her hips and thighs like a dance.
(And when will she cry again?) Peace to the doubt that propels our lives,
peace to the words that will not come back to our mouths,
words like migratory birds that have no Europe, no Africa,
only the Here with this young woman between Gath
and Galon. Here and now and in other days.

6

I went looking for the grave of a man called Menachem, whose name
means consolation, but he died in one place and was buried
in another, far from where he was born.
Years ago we two sat huddled in that dangerous trench,
packing dynamite—its odor nearly choked us,
its almond smell of spring and summer turned into the smell of death.
I went looking for the grave at his kibbutz among the streams of
    the Galilee.
Again I crossed that temporary bridge—each time a vehicle passed
it sounded like metal clanking. But now the bridge is permanent
and quiet, makes not a sound. The dead man, too,
is permanent and quiet. Only I, the living one, I am still
temporary, I make the sounds of life passing.
And with the consolation of his name, Menachem
took preventive measures against death.

7

I ask myself at what speed the force of things past
reaches me. At the speed of melting snows
that flow from Mount Hermon all the way down to the Dead Sea
or of a heavy slow stream of lava from an erupting volcano
or of stalactites dripping in a cavern.
I don't know. On my desk is a broken stone
with "Amen" carved on it, a stone from a Jewish grave of a thousand
     years ago.
It's on my desk now, weighing down papers so they won't fly away.
There it lies—a thing of beauty, a toy of history and fate.
On my desk is a fragment of a hand grenade
that didn't kill me, and there it is—free as a butterfly.

8

Flowing waters always try to teach us something.
Back then we didn't know what they were teaching, but we learned.
Near the water, wild birds in a bush.
Now they all have precise new names
but they go on flying and blossoming and being called
"pretty bird," "sweet-smelling bush." And decisions taken,
and those not taken, are flowing waters:
waters flowing from what has always been
to what will always be.

9

Nineteen forty-eight—that was the year.
Now everything is different here.

Israeli Travel: Otherness Is All,
Otherness Is Love

I

The vineyard in ruins at Petach Tikvah, near the bus co-op
they called "United Fruit of the Land." The fruit was united
and the land was sweet when we were alive and young.
But now the vineyard is old and in ruins, like the vineyards of long ago
where they would tread the grapes to make wine,
and the vineyard wall is just a whitewashed wall for mourning
and forgetting. (Enchanted places are the opiates of my life.)
Nearby there was a big orchard that two of us entered.
The two of us. We came out two others:
he-other and she-other together,
he-lover and she-lover together. And I said to myself,
Otherness is all. Otherness is love.

2

Twilight in Ein HaShofet, "Wellspring of the Judge."
Is Hanan here? Is he still around?
No, he's not. He's gone. Someone else is here. Some other man.
But he was here with me, a scrawny fellow, tall, a chronic cougher,
and when someone coughs you don't say "Bless you!"—you say
    nothing at all.
And where is the wellspring? Dried up like the dead judge,
like Hanan's throat.
And now begins the fanfare about the great mistake.
Which mistake? About Hanan, the wellspring, the judge,
the mistake about sundown. The sun doesn't go down,
we do.

3

A night drive to Ein Yahav in the Arava Desert,
a drive in the rain. Yes, in the rain.
There I met people who grow date palms,
there I saw tamarisk trees and risk trees,

there I saw hope barbed as barbed wire.
And I said to myself: That's true, hope needs to be
like barbed wire to keep out despair,
hope must be a minefield.

4

A picture in color of plowman and horse from the turn of the century
in one of those early settlements in Palestine
hanging on the wall of a summer home in a land far across the sea.
And outside, a luxurious lawn
surrounded by flowers, and on the lawn an empty chair.
And I said to myself: Sit down in this chair, sit here and remember,
sit here and judge—if not, someone else will sit in this chair
to remember and judge. What took place an hour ago
had its place, and what took place on that farm at the turn of
    the century
had its place, and there were trees whose leaves blustered in the wind
and trees that stood by in silence. And the wind
the same wind. In the trees, the bluster and the silence.
And what was and what might have been are as if they never were.
But the wind is the same wind,
the chair is the same chair for remembering and judging,
and the plowman in the picture goes on plowing
what has always been, and sowing
what never will be.

5

I'm the chimp of chance, the champ of chance, I'm a chum of chance
and a chump of chance. When I took off my clothes at night
a coin slipped from my pants pocket onto the floor,
and I didn't know that ringing coin would determine
my fate, perhaps, and the course of my life.

I am the dice in a game of chance, my face up or
my face down. By the way I fall I determine
my own fate and the fate of others.
And I didn't know that my features and the lines on my face
would become a map for someone's travels, or for wars, perhaps,
long after my time.
And he? He won't know either.

6

I remember a problem in a math book
about a train that leaves from place A and another train
that leaves from place B. When will they meet?
No one ever asked what happens when they meet:
Will they stop, or pass each other, or collide?
None of the problems was about a man who leaves from place A
and a woman who leaves from place B. When will they meet,
will they meet at all, and for how long?
As for that math book: Now I've reached
the final pages with the answers.
Back then it was forbidden to look.
Now it is permitted. Now I check
where I was right and where I went wrong,
and know what I did well and what I did not do. Amen.

7

I passed by the school where I studied as a boy
and said in my heart: Here I learned certain things
and not others. All my life I have loved in vain
the things I didn't learn. I am filled with knowledge,
I am an expert on the botany of the tree of knowledge,
good and evil, I know all about its flowering,
the shape of its leaves, the function of its root system, its pests
    and parasites.

I am still studying good and evil, and will go on studying till the
    day I die.
I stood near the school building. This is the room
where we sat and studied. Classroom windows always open
to the future, but in our innocence we thought it was landscape
we were seeing through the window.
The schoolyard was narrow, paved with large stones.
I remember the brief tumult of the two of us
near the rickety steps, the tumult
that was the beginning of a first great love.
Now it outlives us, as if in a museum,
like everything else in Jerusalem.

    8
People were always telling me: "You've got to live
in the real world." I heard it from parents and teachers.
To live in the real world, like a verdict. What terrible sin
could these souls have committed
that their lives in this world should begin with a verdict:
You are sentenced to reality for life.
With no possibility of parole.
The parole is death.

    9
Here in this field, wild oats used to grow. Up above,
clouds like bags under the eyes of the sleepless,
the lust-weary. Millions of years from now,
heavy clouds and heavy bags under the eyes
will be one and the same.
The poet of the psalms said: "The dead praise not the Lord,"
but I say only the dead praise the Lord.
What have we gained? The known becomes the unknown,
and the unknown is known,

72

a barter economy that has no end. Human beings
disseminating seed with their shoes as they walk,
playing the role of the wind, of the birds and the bees,
without knowing it. So what have we gained?
The psalms of thanksgiving and praise.

   10

In Kfar Blum, between the hills of Golan and the hills of Galilee,
my friend told me: "These hills once were seashore,
we are standing on what once was the floor of the sea."
What does that require of us? To be quieter,
more transparent, to turn inward like fossil shells,
to be light and floating as seaweed.
Then we came to Menachemiya, "God Consoles,"
which lived up to its name and consoled us.
We spoke softly, like the soft hills this spring
near the quiet Jordan, under the sign "No One's Here."

Then we headed south. That waterfall on the Jordan River
soothes as it falls. Unlike a human being.
I thought about the power of dammed-up water
and the power of water falling in a torrent,
the power of weeping and the power of restraint,
the power of a woman's hair pulled back like a dancer's
and the power of a woman's hair bursting free and open like a dancer's.
I thought about it all, and when I got home,
I told my children.

   11

Yad Mordechai. Those who fell here
still look out the windows like sick children
who are not allowed outside to play.
And on the hillside, the battle is reenacted

for the benefit of hikers and tourists. Soldiers of thin sheet iron
rise and fall and rise again. The sheet iron dead and those sheet iron lives,
their voices all—sheet iron. And the resurrection of the dead,
sheet iron that clangs and clangs.

And I said to myself: Everyone is attached to his own lament
as to a parachute. Slowly he descends and slowly hovers
till he touches the hard place.

12

I returned to Bat Gallim, on the outskirts of Haifa. Years ago
I visited that neighborhood; now I don't know a soul there.
A death notice with its black border was posted on the wall:
name of dead man and time of funeral—
gone, like him. I saw a notice about the same
dead man on the wall of a kiosk and the trunk of a eucalyptus
I remembered from that time. (The tree itself has forgotten
its homeland, Australia.) By now I am quite familiar with
the dead man's name and the name of his wife and children,
his workplace that sends condolences, and his burial place.
If I linger another day or two in Bat Gallim,
I'll discover that we're related, I'll become
someone else. And then I passed the crumbling casino,
its pleasures scattered, love affairs grown old.
And the swimming pool—such young archaeology—
its plaster like dried-up tears, and cracked like lips.
I went on down to the harbor, thinking: I'm a lucky man—
I will never have to set sail again.

Evening Promenade on
Valley of the Ghosts Street

1

Evening promenade on Valley of the Ghosts Street, German Colony.
Weariness gives way to the pomp of parading
up and down the street—a ritual, almost. The music I hear
from a house I don't know is inside me now
and words not intended for me are the winds I ride
for the rest of my journey, like a sailboat.
In this house, here, my good friend once lived.
Now he's no longer my friend. We grew apart, distant
beyond recognition, like a landscape
that flattens into a map. But the house is still standing
and the door is the same door that opened for me, then closed.
That's how, with some trepidation, a new religion takes shape.
And in this Jerusalem of ours they quickly shush it up,
as adults do when a child speaks among them unawares.

2

People waiting for someone begin to resemble
those who are not waiting anymore. Silence
covers them all. Despair is a lullaby.
And while they are sleeping at night, God violates
the ban of Rabbi Gershom and opens
their souls to read what is written there,
like a letter. In the morning God tucks the letter back in
and licks the envelope shut.
They will never know He has read every word because
He seals the envelope with an artist's hand,
like the military censor.

3

Here is Hulda's house that knew nights of revelry.
The sound of music playing, feet dancing, mouths filled with song.
All those sounds poured out the windows into the quiet night

and swirled around the windowsills
like a river pouring into a great black sea.
In the corners of the rooms, people stood
and jotted down names, addresses, telephone numbers for each other
on memo pads and memorial pads.
They didn't know that what they were writing
was like numbers and names and places carved
onto gravestones, never to be erased. Never to see each other again.
On the door a sign said "Welcome"
in glorious color. It would never say
"Farewell." For how well would they ever fare?

4

The dancers and the danced have all gone now,
the photographers along with the photographed.
The cameras are hidden away in the gloom of closets
and rolls of undeveloped film will remain forever
in the darkrooms of the world. The last to leave
greet the first to pray at dawn—some at the synagogue,
others at the prayer houses of remembering and forgetting.
They have all gone on to their better worlds, not only the dead.
A few remain standing at the crossroads of empty streets
like windsocks at the airport. But each one
is blown a different way, each in the direction of his flight
by his own wind, his own spirit.
Who could have known back then? They were all going
on the same flight, they thought—one way, one destination.

5

Hulda's house still stands in the same place.
But the sounds of holiday parties have since drifted up
and were lost in the heavenly heights, like holy men in Jerusalem
who ascended on high, promised a second coming and never came.

The welcome sign on the door yellows and darkens like autumn leaves.
Names keep changing, names and souls that once were one.
People bound by a pledge or a solemn vow
are bound no longer, and the pledges and vows are free now
to look for new pledgers and vowers.
As for truth and lies, in time
even an old lie yellows and fades like an ancient relic
and looks more reliable than a shiny new truth
with its wet paint.

6

Hulda's house knew plenty in its day and forgot plenty.
To the east, the power station, now without power,
its engines quiet as people, and to the south
the stately convent of silent nuns
not far from the railroad tracks.
Once a day the train still passes, like a conjured spirit.

Summer and the Far End of Prophecy

I

It's summer again at Akhziv Beach and
here we are again. We know how much is required of us
who are heavier than air, heavier than water.
And how much is asked of the birds: They must sing
courtship songs for the silent fish too, and what a burden on beasts
who must roar out the joy of human couples
in one another's arms. And how much is expected of two people
like us, who in their loving must keep and preserve
those who have never been together
or are now apart.

2

Through the window that is not there, we see our children
searching the old ruin for toys they lost yesterday
and turning up broken clay jars from centuries ago.
The chasm between generations fills up with dust and sand,
human bones, animal bones, a multitude of broken vessels.
Broken jars speak the truth. A new jar is the lie of beauty.

3

Twilight sobs down the side of the gray house
and is consoled. The olive trees show each other
the color of their leaves, green and silver, that's all they have.
A wind comes up from the sea and blows through the empty chairs,
turns, turns, doesn't whirl about but blows from one there to another.
"So help us God"—He will help us, help us to more of
the good and the bad, the light and the dark.
The sun changes colors at sunset, like someone
shifting from one language to another, or from song
to speech and from speech to murmurs, then whispers, then silence.
And from the distance, like the sound of a ping-pong game:
belief in one God and blasphemy rally with each other.

4

Two lie together in love on one air mattress
they have inflated together with their own breath. Amen.

5

Oh, the calendar's blank prophecy on the first of the year.
Oh, the memory of beach chairs folded and stacked
in winter, shackled together with an iron chain
like galley slaves in ancient days. Slaves of memory.
Swimmers' strokes preserve the memory of swimming
and of last summer too, of all the summers that were,
swimmers' strokes proceed from love
and unto love they shall return. Oh, the great prophecy
of what is past or what is yet to come.
And there, at the far end of prophecy,
a swimsuit spread out to dry.

6

On the way back to Jerusalem we stopped at Aqua Bella,
the valley of beautiful waters. We sat in the shade of a Crusader
    fortress,
but it was not a fortress, it was a convent
whose nuns donated their love to us. How can we rest
with this burden weighing on our love?
The flowers near the water are pledges and vows
that grace our lives with their colors
and their desperate perfume. And in the rush of the beautiful waters
the vows come undone, undone, undone.

7

The memorial forest where we made love
burned down in a great conflagration

but the two of us stayed alive and in love
in memory of the burnt forest
and in memory of the burnt ones the forest remembered.

Houses (Plural); Love (Singular)

1

Sheltered by good news,
sheltered even by the bad, now we are at home.
But we remain as we were then, before we had a home,
when we were in the wadis of Ein Gedi. We are still
like those wadis, you the Rejeh, I the Sideir, even now,
sheltered in our home in Jerusalem. At our door
the two eunuchs, Time and Fate, stand guard,
and the mezuzah on our doorpost says:
And thou, man, shalt love;
and thou, woman, shalt love.

2

We lived in many houses and left remnants of memory
in every one of them: a newspaper, a book face-down, a crumpled map
of some faraway land, a forgotten toothbrush standing sentinel in
    a cup—
that too is a memorial candle, an eternal light.

3

And in those days before we made a home for ourselves,
we made the whole country into homes.
Even the beach at Caesarea
where we piled our clothes onto a solemn mound,
sandals and shirts and towels and pants, yours and mine,
jumbled together, like us, and then went into the water.
I said to myself: If we'd lived in ancient times and made love
in the mountains or the desert, we'd have piled stone on stone
and called upon the name of the Lord and gone on our way,
but we made love by the sea, our clothes
a mound of witness in the sand,
and we called upon the name of our love.
Passersby thought we might have drowned in the sea.

But we did not drown in the sea, we drowned in all the years
after that chapter, still wrapped up
in each other, like our clothes on that mound on the shore.

   4

We lived in the Valley of Gehenna in no man's land in the divided
   Jerusalem.
Our roof was hit, our walls wounded by bullets and shrapnel.
We propped up the broken leg of the bed with a pile of books.
(I don't know if we ever read them again.) The stone steps
were like the ladder the angels left behind when they fled
Jacob's dream, a ladder for us to climb up and down.
In Hebrew, no man's land is called "the zone of abandon."
When we lived there, we were a man and a woman earnest in our loving,
we were not abandoned. And if we have not died, we are loving still.

   5

And if we have died, we will be first in line at the resurrection
that Ezekiel prophesied in his vision:
bones coming together, bone to bone, skin over flesh and sinew—
Ezekiel didn't go into detail. But the two of us continued his vision:
hips for hugging, soft inner thighs for stroking, twin buttocks, upper
and nether hair, eyes to open and close, lips chiseled, the tongue precise.
And we fleshed out his vision even further:
two people talking, a summer dress, underwear hung out to dry,
   a windowsill.
We will be ourselves, we will be ebb and flow, changing weathers,
seasons of the year, we will go on being,
we will go on and on.

The Language of Love
and Tea with Roasted Almonds

I

Layla, night, the most feminine of all things, is masculine
in Hebrew, but it is also the name of a woman.
Sun is masculine and sunset feminine,
the memory of the masculine in the feminine, and the yearning
of a woman in a man. That is to say: the two of us, that is to say: we.
And why is *Elohim,* God, in the plural? Because All of Him
are sitting in the shade under a canopy of vines in Akko,
playing cards. And we sat at a table nearby and I held your hand
and you held mine instead of cards, and we too
were masculine and feminine, plural and singular,
and we drank Arab tea with roasted almonds, two tastes
that didn't know each other and became one in our mouth.
And over the café door, next to the sky, it said:
"Not Responsible for Items Forgotten or Lost."

2

Near the cemetery you always find stonecutters and gardeners.
Near the courthouse, lawyers' offices and phone booths.
Near hope, plenty of despair, and around the train station, hotels.
And in the neighborhood of love, words like "I love you,"
"I love you too," more binding than any marriage vow.
It's not enough to say "Behold, thou art fair, my love,"
you have to say "I love" seven times,
just as you say "The Lord is God" seven times
in the prayer of Closing the Gates on Yom Kippur
and when the gates of life are closing.
And there's all that talk about Till death do us part,
Even death will not part us, it will bind us
somewhere in the universe
in a new encounter that has no end.

3

Lovers leave fingerprints on each other,
plenty of physical evidence, words without end, testimonies, a wrinkled
pair of pants, a newspaper with the exact date, and two watches, his
    and hers.
Every morning they trace each other's contours
the way the police mark the location of the body on the road
with chalk. Lovers surrender each other,
lovers reserve the right to remain silent.
If and when they are separated,
they compose a police sketch of their faces and a lineup
so they can say: He's the one! She's the one!

4

I know a man who assembled an ideal woman
from all his desires: the hair he took
from a woman in the window of a passing bus,
the forehead from a cousin who died young, the hands
from a teacher he had as a boy, the cheeks from a little girl,
his childhood love, the mouth from a woman he noticed
in a phone booth, the thighs from a woman lying on the beach,
the alluring gaze from this one, the eyes from that one,
the waistline from a newspaper ad. From all these he assembled
a woman he truly loved. And when he died, they came,
all the women—legs chopped off, eyes plucked out, faces slashed
    in half,
hands severed, hair ripped out, a gash where a mouth used to be,
and demanded what was theirs, theirs, theirs,
dismembered his body, tore his flesh, and left him
only his misbegotten soul.

5

Now they will begin to tell the things we've done together
and the places we've been, as compared with the places
we haven't, the things we have not done and will never do.
A two-part harmony will accompany us
like two different choirs on each side of our lives,
or like the two camps that assembled—one on the Mount of Blessings
and one on the Mount of Curses. Sometimes even
in a quiet conversation between two people at the next table,
or in the way names and times and places are announced at the airport.
And sometimes the voices are within us
like a confession: Yes, we were, yes, we did,
yes, we lingered for a while, no, we were not, we did not.
Like a confession trilled out on Yom Kippur. And that
is all of eternity that we shall know.

6

Imagine that when you and I are driving in this car,
the entire factory rides along: engineers
and workers, the assembly line, the noise of the machines,
oil wells down in their depths, geologic faults,
even the formation of planet earth.
Now that's the way to love!

7

The way a photographer, when he sets up
a shot of sea or desert out to the edge of the horizon,
has to get something large and close-up into the picture—
a branch, a chair, a boulder, the corner of a house,
to get a sense of the infinite, and he forgets about the sea
and the desert—that's how I love you, your hand,

your face, your hair, your nearby voice,
and I forget the everlasting distance and the endless endings.
And when we die, again there will be only sea and desert
and the God we so loved to look at from the window.
Peace, peace to the far and the near, to the true Gods, peace.

    8

Thus have lovers preeminence above all others:
others may say "Take my place"
but lovers actually keep their word.
Now I am in your place, and you in mine. You are me, I am you.
Everything has changed; nothing has changed. Only the places.
The others. Sometimes people argue "You're
just using me," "you're taking advantage."
But lovers say the very same words with joy, with passion:
"I want it, take advantage of me," "I
want it too—use me
up."

    9

In the faint light on the balcony of an old house in Barcelona
one summer night, I saw a man and a woman.
In the room behind them, a white bed shining in the bright light.
Downstairs, their names in the dark, near the gate, like mezuzahs,
and ancient names whispered over their sleek taut skin, like a breeze.

    10

Every woman in love has the face of the Virgin Mary, mother of Jesus,
in the pietàs. She remembers what happened to another woman
in another time, she remembers even what has not
happened yet, the future already belongs
to her memory. Pain and joy yoked together.
She knows about the death of the dead man as he lies in her arms,

and she knows about the resurrection of the dead in her arms.
She too is the precision of pain and the blurriness of joy.

11

What shall we do with the wonderfully sly story
of David and Jonathan? "Behold, the arrows are beyond thee,"
said Jonathan. But where? Over there,
there, a bit to the left. But where exactly? As in a children's game:
cold, colder, getting warm, warmer, hot, right there.
What shall we do with that old story now, in our own day?
One generation handed it down to the next in the synagogue reading
on the Sabbath before the new moon—"Tomorrow is the feast
of the new moon," said Jonathan. Handed it down like a beautiful
sad glass dome with David and Jonathan inside
till it fell from empty hands and shattered.
Ours is the age of the mender, the healer and the restorer,
but it is the two of us, you and I,
who will fill in the missing pieces when we love.

12

Every woman in love is like our mother Sarah,
lying in wait behind the door while the men inside
discuss the beauty of her body and her future.
She laughs into her palm, her hollow palm, as into a womb,
ocarina of a future, like the light cough of a clever fox.
Every woman making love is Rachel and Leah trading off
body and soul between them, seasons and dresses, kohl and perfumes,
the tastes of day flavored with the spices of night,
night stirrings with day sounds, thighs and breasts, to become one body,
Rachel and Leah, Racheleah. It's as if Jacob were in bed with two
    women,
one stormy and fiery, knowing she will die soon in childbirth,
the other placid and soft and heavy, down the generations

till me. And the face of every woman when she's loving
is like the face of the moon in its cycle,
full-face in the door as it opens and half-face by the window.
And every loving woman is like Rebecca at the well, saying
"Drink, and thy camels also." But in our day Rebecca says:
"The towels are on the top shelf in the white closet
across from the front door."

The Precision of Pain and the Blurriness of Joy:
The Touch of Longing Is Everywhere

I

I sit in my friends' garden on a chair made of hollow
bamboo reeds. Other reeds were turned into flutes to be played
in other places. I sit at ease, I sit shiva for time lost
and time that will be lost, and my heart is calm and quiet.
The spirits of the dead visit me in the light of day
and the spirits of the living haunt my nights.
I sit on a chair made of bamboo reeds
that wanted to be flutes, just as the flutes would have liked
to be calm and quiet in a chair. I think about bamboo reeds
that grow near the water. There's longing everywhere.
The precision of pain and the blurriness of joy.

2

In my garden I saw jasmine blossoms carried by the autumn wind,
clinging to the bougainvillea. Oh, what a mistake, what a waste,
what a loss to no end. I saw a sun setting in the sea,
I saw God, what a mistake, what a hope!
I saw two birds caught in the lofty halls
of an airport. In despair they flew over the chaos below.
Oh, what a mistake, what a flight, what a desperate love,
what a way out without an out, what a vision of the Shekhinah's wings!
And high up, above it all, a plane is circling. I'm trying, it says,
I'm trying again. Try, they tell it
from the control tower. Try again, try again.

3

Each year the melons are sweeter than the year before.
Is it forgetting last summer that makes me say this
or some great weariness? When a voice gets worn out
it grows sweeter. Even hoarseness is like white sugar,
and seedless melons are the sweetest of all.
"Let not the eunuch say, Behold, I am a dry tree"—thus the prophet,

long ago, consoled those who have no offspring
and never will. Even seed spilled on the ground
may one day sow a human being.
Comfort ye, comfort ye, Er and Onan, you will be resurrected yet.

   4

I saw a yellowing photo of Jaffa, from the time
before I was born, and in the photo a tower
and on the tower a clock, and on the clock: quarter to six.
The tower was precise and the time precise.
O, dirges of the hours, weep ye for all the seven o'clocks that will
      not return,
grieve for the lost half past twos, woe for the six o'clocks
that were gathered unto the hours in their prime,
in my prime, a bitter wailing for all the hours that have passed away,
an elegy for the good times, a hallelujah howling for the bad.
Mourn ye quarter to six. Mourn quarter past six. Even half hours
and quarter hours will find perfect rest
in the ascension of ordained times and memorials
under the wings of forgetting.

   5

To erect a monument in the wrong place, like the Tomb of Rachel,
to call someone by the wrong name, to say words that were not meant
to miss or to hit, to move things from one spot to another,
stones from the quarry to the construction site,
to pump water into pipes, to surprise, to change—
these are the true longings.
When a window curtain wants to be a flag outside,
when the past wants to be the future,
when tears yearn not for laughter, nor for the eyes
that wept them, nor for the cheeks they wet,
but for the sea, for the salt in the sea—these are the true longings.

6

At a pay phone, I saw a woman making a call,
and crouching at her feet, a large musical instrument in a black case,
   like a dog.

7

I think about the joy of clothing in the store window
that no one has bought, and the joy
of furniture that has not been sold,
but I also think about the sadness of the clothes and the furniture
and about their longing to be inside rooms with human beings
to sense the warmth of their bodies.

8

We remember the past
and God remembers the future.
Then we forget the past,
God forgets the future,
and the world returns to chaos.

9

Sometimes my soul wants to get out of my body for a little run,
like a dog, and return calmer to the body. But it worries
that it won't find the way back.

10

Godforsaken people meet godforsaking people;
people who forsake their childhood love those who remember.
Both have straps of every kind on their clothing, straps fastened tight
to support them and their souls on their journeys.

11

King Saul fell upon his sword in the last battle on Mount Gilboa
and died at once. So too we fall upon
our sharp-edged souls when we are born,
but we die only seventy or eighty years later.
All those years, life writhes within us, every motion
and emotion pierces deep, but we grow used to the pain.
Sometimes we call it feeling alive, even joy.
The soul that quickens us kills us in the end
and lodges there, like the sword.

12

When the sun sets in the west, the hope of the night rises red in me.
So too, with the security of a seesaw, we tell about the things we did,
the places we saw. Even wars and loves
steady us and give us that seesaw security, the up-down
of whatever was.

13

In a Jerusalem courtyard I saw seeds
spread on a cloth to dry in the sun, and I said:
Let me be their historian and tell them about the watermelons
and pumpkins they came from. I insist that the sand
remember the stone, that the stone remember the great rock
and the rock—the lava and the fire.
And I myself forget what took place last summer,
even what took place yesterday, which happened to be
a Wednesday. But I remember
the psalm the Levites would sing each week
in the Temple on Wednesday.

14

Longings are the fruit.
Words and deeds that truly happen
are the flowers of the field that wither and fade.
The fruit remains a while longer, bearing the seeds of longings to come.
The root lasts, deep in the ground.

15

And all the while messengers keep running back and forth
to my childhood to retrieve what I forgot or left behind
as if from a house that is about to be demolished,
or like Robinson Crusoe, from the slowly sinking ship
to the island—so I salvage from my childhood provisions and memories
for the next installment of my life.

16

The precision of pain and the blurriness of joy. I'm thinking
how precise people are when they describe their pain in a doctor's office.
Even those who haven't learned to read and write are precise:
"This one's a throbbing pain, that one's a wrenching pain,
this one gnaws, that one burns, this is a sharp pain
and that—a dull one. Right here. Precisely here,
yes, yes." Joy blurs everything. I've heard people say
after nights of love and feasting, "It was great,
I was in seventh heaven." Even the spaceman who floated
in outer space, tethered to a spaceship, could say only, "Great,
wonderful, I have no words."
The blurriness of joy and the precision of pain—
I want to describe, with a sharp pain's precision, happiness
and blurry joy. I learned to speak among the pains.

In My Life, on My Life

1

All my life I played chess with myself and with others
and the days of my life were chess pieces, good and bad—I and me,
I and he, war and love, hope and despair,
black pieces and white. Now they're all jumbled together,
colorless, and the chessboard has no squares,
it's a smooth surface blending into night and into day.
The game is calm and has no end, no winners,
no losers, the hollow rules
clang in the wind. I listen. And I am quiet.
In my life and in my death.

2

When I was a boy I said the bedtime prayer
every night. I remember the verse
"The angel who delivers me from all danger."
I never prayed after that, not on my bed,
not in the hills, not in war, not by day and not by night,
but the delivering angel stayed by my side and became
a loving angel. That loving angel will turn into the Angel of Death
when the hour comes, but it is always the same angel
who delivers me from all danger.

3

I always have to revisit the sands of Ashdod
where I had a little bit of courage in that battle, that war,
soft hero in the soft sand. My few scraps of heroism I squandered then,
that's why I always revisit the sands of Ashdod. Now they've become
vacation sands—swimmers, children at play,
warning flags, a lifeguard. In those days
there were no warning flags, no guard, no one to save us.

4

I always have to revisit the ticklings of my childhood,
the ticklings I used to get from my aunts back when it was
an act of grace, true grace. For the sheer joy of living.
Since then, tickling has become a serious business, no longer the ringing
laughter of a child: a tickle verging on pain, new skin healing the breach
between good and evil, a tickle of wild passion and resurrection.
Sometimes I send my hand all the way up to my scalp to scratch
like a rocket launched into light-years of space—my head at the edge of
    the galaxy.
Sometimes in the morning I rub my eyes lightly, toward my nose,
toward the soothing, saving work of memory.
That motion conjures spirits from the magic-trick-bag
of the body, the generations of tickles. And best of all,
that sensation when my thigh grows indifferent and goes to sleep,
then suddenly jerks awake with a million exquisite pins and needles.
Thus a new religion begins after an age of apathy:
out of the blue a new tickle, a new faith. Amen selah.

5

I know how slight are the threads that tie me to my joy
but from those slight threads I have woven strong clothing,
a kind of soft armor, the warp and weft of joy
to help me cover my nakedness and protect me.
But sometimes it seems to me my life isn't worth
the skin of my body that wraps around it, not even
these fingernails with which I hang on to my life.
I am like a man who holds his wrist up
to catch a glimpse of Time, even when he isn't wearing a watch.
And sometimes the gurgling of the last waters
draining from the bathtub
is a nightingale's song to my ear.

6

The world is filled with remembering and forgetting
like sea and dry land. Sometimes memory
is the solid ground we stand on,
sometimes memory is the sea that covers all things
like the Flood. And forgetting is the dry land that saves, like Ararat.

7

I want my brain not to be inside my head
but in some other part of my body—my feet, my belly,
my buttocks, an intense little cerebellum in my navel.
Or even outside my body—let my brain be a hollow
scooped in the sand, where donkeys, dogs and children
roll around, tumble and squeal with delight.
On my life, I swear it: that's what I want in my life, on my life!

8

And every person is a dam between past and future.
When he dies the dam bursts, the past breaks into the future,
and there is no before or after. All time becomes one time
like our God: our Time is One.
Blessed be the memory of the dam.

9

Life is called life as the west wind is called
west, though it blows toward the east.
The way death is called death, though it blows toward life.
In a cemetery we remember the living, and outside it—
the dead. As the past leads to the future
though it's called past, as you to me and I to you in love
though I'm called by my name and you by yours.

As spring provides for summer, as summer beds down into fall.
As my thoughts will be till the end of my life. That is the banner of
   my God.

   10
When a man dies, they say "He was gathered unto his fathers."
As long as he is alive, his fathers are gathered within him,
each cell of his body and soul a delegate from one of his
thousands of fathers since the beginning of time.

   11
Each day now I hear the circles of my life closing,
the click of buckles, like kisses
of conciliation and love. And these lend a rhythm
to the latest version of my life. Things that were lost long ago
find their places now, like billiard balls, each one into its pocket.
Contracts and prophecies are fulfilled, prophecies true and false.
I come upon the missing lids of pots and pans that stayed uncovered,
I find the matching pieces, like an ancient contract of clay
broken into two parts, unequal but fitting together.
Like a mosaic, like a jigsaw puzzle, children searching
for the missing pieces. When the game is over,
the picture will be whole. Complete.

   12
I, may I rest in peace—I, who am still living, say,
May I have peace in the rest of my life.
I want peace right now while I'm still alive.
I don't want to wait like that pious man who wished for one leg
of the golden chair of Paradise, I want a four-legged chair
right here, a plain wooden chair. I want the rest of my peace now.
I have lived out my life in wars of every kind: battles without
and within, close combat, face-to-face, the faces always

my own, my lover-face, my enemy-face.
Wars with the old weapons—sticks and stones, blunt axe, words,
dull ripping knife, love and hate,
and wars with newfangled weapons—machine gun, missile,
words, land mines exploding, love and hate.
I don't want to fulfill my parents' prophecy that life is war.
I want peace with all my body and all my soul.
Rest me in peace.

13

When I die, I want only women to handle me in the Chevra Kadisha
and to do with my body as they please: cleanse my ears of the last
words I heard, wipe my lips of the last words I said,
erase the sights I saw from my eyes, smooth my brow of worries
and fold my arms across my chest like the sleeves of a shirt after ironing.
Let them salve my flesh with perfumed oil to anoint me King of Death
for a day, and arrange in my pelvic basin as in a fruit bowl
testes and penis, navel and frizzy hair—like an ornate still life
from some past century, a very still life on a ground of dark velvet,
and then with a feather tickle my mouth-hole and asshole to check
if I'm still alive. Let them laugh and cry by turns
and administer a last massage that passes from their hands through me
to the entire world till the End of Days.
And one of them will sing God Full of Mercy,
will sing in a sweet voice God Full of Womb,
to remind God that mercy is born of the womb, true mercy,
true womb, true love, true grace. On my life, I swear it,
that's what I want in my death, in my life.

Jewish Travel: Change Is God
and Death Is His Prophet

I

Jewish travel. As it is written, "I will lift up mine eyes unto the hills,
from whence cometh my help": not a hike to see a tall mountain in
    all its glory,
nor a climb to rejoice in the vistas of Nature,
but a hike with a purpose, to seek help from the high heavens.
And how to interpret "I will lift up mine eyes"? Heavy Jewish eyes
that need lifting. And it is written, "Who shall ascend the mountain
    of the Lord?"
Not hikers singing, knapsacks on their shoulders, but rather
a congregation praying with "clean hands and a pure heart,"
not strong bodies and sturdy legs. And fertile valleys
are simply good places for prayer: as it says, "Out of the depths
have I cried unto thee, O Lord." Even "green pastures"
and "still waters" are not about resting and eating in the shade of a tree
or camping near a stream in the scorch of summer,
but about praising the Lord, since right after that it says
"the Valley of the Shadow of Death"—
the shadow of death overshadows everything. Jewish travel.
Even Moses climbed Mount Sinai not as mountaineers do,
but to receive the Tablets of the Law. And he went up Mount Nebo
not to come down again but to die.

2

Yehuda Halevi wrote, "In the East is my heart, and I dwell at the end
    of the West."
That's Jewish travel, that's the Jewish game of hearts between east
    and west,
between self and heart, to and fro, to without fro, fro without to,
fugitive and vagabond without sin. An endless journey, like the trip
Freud the Jew took, wandering between body and mind, between
mind and mind, only to die between the two.
Oh, what a world this is, where the heart is in one place and the body

117

in another (almost like a heart torn from a body and transplanted).
I think about people who are named for a place where they have
      never been
and will never be. Or about an artist who draws a man's face
from a photograph because the man is gone. Or about the migration
      of Jews,
who do not follow summer and winter, life and death
as birds do, but instead obey the longings of the heart. That's why
they are so dead, and why they call their God *Makom*, "Place."
And now that they have returned to their place, the Lord has taken up
wandering to different places, and His name will no longer be Place
but Places, Lord of the Places.
Even the resurrection of the dead is a long journey.
What remains? The suitcases on top of the closet,
that's what remains.

3

Moses standing on Mount Nebo was the first
to say in his heart, "In the West is my heart, and I
am at the end of the East," but he also said,
"In the East is my heart, and I am at the end of the West."
Thus began the long voyage, the great Jewish journey.
Mount Nebo was the watershed where his longings divided.
He yearned for the land of Canaan he would never see,
but he turned east, toward the desert of those forty years,
and wrote the Torah as a travel book,
a memoir, every chapter with something very personal
that was his alone—like Pharaoh's daughter, like his sister Miriam,
his brother Aaron, his black wife, the Ten Commandments.

4

Moses went into training in preparation for the long trek in the desert.
He staged a reconnaissance mission to the burning bush,

trained the pillar of fire and the pillar of smoke, then returned to Egypt
to arrange a dress rehearsal for the exodus. He practiced each move
like an acrobat, till the miracle rod felt natural in his hands.
In maneuvers with live ammunition, people sometimes get killed.
There are those who consult a map before a long march
and those who check later: "This is where I walked,
that's where I was." And there is the grief before, and the grief after.
And Jesus the Jew staged a reconnaissance mission to Golgotha,
to the Valley of Gethsemane and up the Via Dolorosa.
He inspected his Jewish burial place, measured it,
tested the weight of the gravestones, what the weather was like,
and how deep the pit from which he would rise, a Christ.

5

Every year our father Abraham would take his sons to Mount Moriah
the way I take my children to the Negev hills where I once had a war.
Abraham hiked around with his sons. "This is where I left
the servants behind, that's where I tied the donkey to a tree
at the foot of the mountain, and here, right here, Isaac my son,
    you asked:
Behold the fire and the wood, but where is the lamb for a burnt
    offering?
Then, up a little further, you asked for the second time."
When they reached the mountaintop, they rested a bit, ate and drank,
and he showed them the thicket where the ram was caught by its horns.

After Abraham died, Isaac started taking his sons to the same place.
"Here I lifted the wood, this is where I got out of breath,
here I asked, and my father answered: God will see to the lamb
for the offering. Over there, I already knew it was me."
And when Isaac's eyes were dim with age, his children
led him to that same spot on Mount Moriah, and recounted for him
all that had come to pass, all that he might have forgotten.

6

We no longer ask: Where has the sun disappeared to, whence
does the moon rise, where did my father go, where is God,
whither is thy beloved gone. Our questions are cunning and concealed
like baited fishhooks: Where is that man who was here a moment ago,
when do the latitudes cross the longitudes—all a nudge and a wink
at death. Where is Palmach Street. Where is the street
that used to be Palmach Street. Where is the Palmach
they turned into a street, and the street they turned into a crossroad.
What remains? Move and countermove.
When they meet, they create turbulence. East and west will never meet,
like the two halves of a tunnel that is badly planned.
What remains? The sense of expansion and the sense of contraction,
expansion like a night of stars,
contraction like a mouth puckering at the taste of lemon.
What was and what might have been.
Deeds and the empty gestures of deeds along the roadside
like rows of trees lining the boulevard.

7

In the museum in St. Petersburg, they found a Jewish marriage contract
from the seventeenth century. It had a golden border
of peacocks and does, not an image of bride and groom. The lettering
has not faded, nor have the illuminations; today that *ketubah*
is more valuable than the memory of the couple.
The voice of the bridegroom and the voice of the bride
were silenced and forgotten in the smoke-and-mirror halls of time.
Did he tell her "I love you" before
he said "Behold, thou art sanctified unto me"
or after? And what is in the space between "I love"
and "Behold, thou art"? What grows there, what rustles and hums,
what is whispered, what remains, what of the night?

The suitcases on top of the closet, that's what remains,
like empty coffins.

   8

Jewish travel of another kind: with my wife and children
I went to the remote German village where my grandmother
was born. The house with its red roof is still there,
the stream at the edge of the garden still streaming,
the fertile flower beds between house and stream.
In those flower beds I would have liked to plant choirs of children,
mouths open like snapdragons for a mournful song.
Here grandmother the girl picked mulberries and raspberries.
Someday, in another faraway time, these may be new names
for new children: Mulberry, Mulberella, Raspberry, Raspberitte.
Then shall the song of that mournful choir be thanksgiving and praise.
And my grandmother is buried on the cruel dry Mount of Olives
from which the olives have retreated—it is a stone mountain,
a grave-mountain. There she lies buried
and the memory of the streaming water and the mulberries
lies buried with her.

   9

On a little hill amid fertile fields lies a small cemetery,
a Jewish cemetery behind a rusty gate, hidden by shrubs,
abandoned and forgotten. Neither the sound of prayer
nor the voice of lamentation is heard there,
for the dead praise not the Lord.
Only the voices of our children ring out, seeking graves and cheering
each time they find one—like mushooms in the forest, like wild
    strawberries.
Here's another grave! There's the name of my mother's
mothers, and a name from the last century. And here's a name,

and there! And as I was about to brush the moss from the name—
Look! an open hand engraved on the tombstone, the grave of a *kohen*,
his fingers splayed in a spasm of holiness and blessing,
and here's a grave concealed by a thicket of berries
that has to be brushed aside like a shock of hair
from the face of a beautiful beloved woman.

10

Then we came to a ritual bath in ruins. A good man led us to it
as if it were one of those hidden shrines in the jungles of Burma
   or Mexico.
For fifty years that ruined *mikveh* lay covered with a thicket of thorns,
not a soul to uproot it. The rain
that once gathered into a pool of purifying waters
has not stopped falling, but there is no pool now, no purifying.
Where a mirror once hung on the wall, there is a raspberry bush,
and in place of the Jewish woman who gazed into that mirror, ferns
grow wild. And where vapors rose from the pools of water
and from the skin of the women immersing themselves, the nettle grows
and the ivy, the vapors became witnesses of death, the women
died in the cycle of impurity and purity and fire, in the cycle of change
and Otherness. Speak O my soul, Change is God.
The cycle is all: the cycle of blood in the body, the cycle of water,
of prayers for the holy days. Speak O my soul, sing
O my soul, to the God who is Himself part of the cycle
of praise and lament, curse and blessing.
Speak O my soul, sing O my soul, Change is God
and death is His prophet.

11

And at dusk, in the last light of day, we saw
a small soccer field in a forest clearing:

the chalk lines had long since faded, and there were no boundaries,
  no rules,
no regulations. Dead soccer players were playing, invisible,
and the whistle shrieked like keening women.
The goalposts were the Gate of Justice at one end
and the Gate of Mercy at the other. The nets were torn,
the souls of the dead slipped through.
And in the middle of the field, a soccer ball, black and white,
was the only real thing in the grass, as if left there from those
  other days.

12

At night I walked again along the row of weeping willows
whose branches reach down. I sat on the same bench
where I waited many years ago, when I was a little boy.
Two generations of remembering have passed,
now the first generation of forgetting has come. The circle
was closed, the circle was broken. But there I was again, sitting
  and waiting
near the weeping willows, sitting and waiting for the man, for the other.
Tears drew silver threads from the streetlight to my eyes.
If there are weeping willows there ought to be
joyful willows and hoping willows too, whose branches reach up.
(And when was the last time you cried?) Rings in a tree trunk reveal
how old the tree is, as tears tell the length of a human life.
And when was the last time you cried?

13

He stepped out of the car. I offered him water.
Where had he come from, I asked, and where was he going this time,
did all of this really need to be. He answered, his voice
unsteady, "I am in transit, I have been traveling, I am in the cycle

of departure and return, I come from those other days
and I am headed toward those other days. But the Now is always
    with me."
He took a sip, handed me the cup, and said: "They have built
a small temple where the great old synagogue used to be.
The new temple is modern and shiny, air-conditioned, the seats
are comfortable, the partition of the women's section
is made of expensive fabric, an artistic design, but there is no
minyan for prayer and no women in the women's section.
Nor should you forget the red memorial light, the eternal
flame—that incurable inflammation of the Jewish people.
Now they have built a modern *mikveh* on the ruins of the old one,
and the walls are made of marble, the faucets solid-gold-plate,
with sweat rooms and fitness corners. But there are
hardly any women left, and those who remain
have no need of a *mikveh*. Their cycle is over. Finished."

   14
"And now I must leave again. I must return
to the cycle of remembering and forgetting. Farewell. We will meet
someday." Thus he spoke and turned away from me.
I followed him to the black car, the car
drove off. He drove off, he was gone.
What remains? The suitcases on top of the closet—
they are all that remains, like suitcases
floating on the water after a ship goes down.
Until they too—

   15
Once I said, Death is God and change is His prophet.
Now I have calmed down, and I say:
Change is God and death is His prophet.

124

Names, Names, in Other Days
and in Our Time

1

My name is Yehúda. The stress on the *hu,*
Yehu, yoo-hoo——a mother's voice calling her little boy in from play,
who who, a voice that crieth from the wilderness, who who,
a voice that crieth unto the wilderness. A surprising *yoo* and a
    surprised *hoo,*
a long-drawn-out who of the loves of my life.

My name is Yehudá, the stress on the *da,*
Yehudá like "thank you" in Hebrew, *todá,* a Yehudean pride,
relic of the heroics of Judah the Maccabee.
Yehudá like a resounding oud——a dull echo
like a string wrapped around a pack of letters,
or a sharp echo like an elastic band snapping
at a woman's waist. *Da da,* no Yehu, no Yahweh,
but a daring plunge with a wide-open parachute into a wedding,
down through the atmospheric layers of my life.

2

My name is Yehuda, but those who love me call me Yuda
as old Jews used to be called, like Grandpa's brother.
Yuda. *Yoo-yoo* a child calls out from his hiding place,
yoo of longings, *yoo-yoo* a ship's foghorn,
yoo yowling or *hoo* hailing Hallelujah, *yoo-yah* Hallelujah.
Yoo from the depths and *hoo* from the heights,
you and who together in the chambers of love.

3

Meir Mindlin divorced his name three times,
went back to his first name and left the country. In his empty flat
many years ago I loved a great love
because a flat cannot tolerate a void: *horror vacui.*
I don't remember in which war I first met him

and in which history, public or private.
He knew five languages, but when the stroke hit him
he was paralyzed, struck dumb in all five tongues.
I want to cleanse his death notice of all the other news on the page
the way archaeologists scrub a clay pot, or the way
a dead body is cleansed of every impurity.
I want to advertise his life—false advertising
for an item that's out of stock, you can't get it anymore.
I want rites of mourning, rending of clothes, shoes slipped off
lightly, easily, like cursing, because curses are light.
It's the blessings that weigh you down.

4

Tova's brother, whom I carried wounded from the battle at Tel Gath,
recovered and was forgotten because he recovered, and died
in a car crash a few years later, and was forgotten
because he died. And even if my bloodied hands
had been prophets then, my eyes saw not
and my feet knew not what the grain in the field knows,
that green wheat ripens yellow.
That's the life prophecy of a field of wheat.

I howl *Hoshana*, O save us! I weep, I implore on Hoshana Rabba.
That howl ripens into beautiful music—in the church choir
it is almost a psalm of praise, Hosanna, Hallelujah,
praise the Lord who did not save.
But I go back to a weepy pleading *Hoshana*
that turns my mouth into a gaping wound
and may soothe me yet, like an infant crying itself to sleep.

5

Abraham Rubinstein arrived at our school in Jerusalem
in 1937, a quiet dark-eyed boy from Lithuania. We

had a party for him when he came. That same year
our voices began to change like the seasons, like a summer and winter
that will never return in the cycle of voices,
back when first loves stirred up a first disorder in our souls
like the mess in the closet or on the table.
In 1938 he returned with his family to Lithuania and we had a party
for him when he left, fun and games, as we did when he came.
If he had stayed in Jerusalem, he would have changed his old Jewish name
to a proud Hebrew name: Rubinstein would have turned into
Ruby, Stone, Diamond, Sapphire,
any gem would do, no matter what color, any name is a good name.
But he went back to Lithuania and I never heard his adult voice,
whole, final, howling in the death camp.
He didn't get to the enchanted places, in life or in death.
And now they come together—what might have been
and whatever was—and the two become one,
like the long-drawn-out "one" at the end
of *Shema Yisrael.* Hear O Israel: The End.

6

Dan Omer—a rebel in life and in death. Even his pitch-black beard
was a rebel, never soft or submissive, never resigned to its fate.
In the end, his own heart rose up against him and killed him from within.
A man of many new beginnings. But even a multitude
of new beginnings comes to a single end. He died
in a hospital called Gates of Justice. All his life he tried to storm
the gates of justice. (Now that old hospital building has also
fallen into decay.) Sometimes I see his aged father still walking
the streets of Jerusalem, head erect, meticulously dressed,
in his hand a dignified walking stick, not just a cane to lean on.
He swings it with the elegance of a Europe gone by.
Inside that walking stick is the soul of his dead son Dan,
like a narrow saber concealed in the cane of a secret agent,

and he doesn't even know it. I am the only one who knows,
because Dan was my friend.

7

Paul Celan. Toward the end, the words grew
fewer inside you, each word
so heavy in your body
that God set you down like a heavy load
for a moment, perhaps, to catch
His breath and wipe His brow.
Then He left you and picked up a lighter load,
another poet. But the last bubbles
that rose from your drowning mouth
were the final concentration, the frothy concentrate
of the heaviness of your life.

8

Louis Rappaport died of a heart attack.
The best father in the world to his four children.
Father of the little girl who sang in the school chorus,
her mouth wide open like a chick in the nest
for the food that papa would bring, and out came a song
wonderfully sweet.

Then one day that good father suddenly died
and now he's become a cautionary tale, the moral of a story
for less perfect children of less perfect fathers:
"Don't upset Papa, you'll give him a heart attack."
But Louis Rappaport was the best father of all.

And from now on we'll need a dispensation to rejoice
like the dispensation to pray on Yom Kippur:
Our sorrow is no sorrow, our weeping no weeping,
our dead are not dead, our despair is no despair.

We permit ourselves to rejoice with the joyous,
to love with the lovers, and to pass with those who pass away.

9

One man's parents gave him an old-fashioned name from the Diaspora.
These days only very old, very praying Jews still go by such a name.
His friends gave him a wild name, because he grew up
to be a big brave paratrooper, raised horses
out in the world and came back to raise them in the hills of Galilee.
His parents own a shop of women's undergarments, corsets for the
    stout ones,
lightweight bras and little silk panties for the lean ones.
And whoever laughs at the story of a generation gap like that,
whoever even cracks a smile, doesn't know a thing about
wild horses or the names of the land of Canaan or Diaspora names
or the hills of Galilee or women
or women's garments, either under or over,
or the land of Israel, or the history of the people of Israel.

10

Ruth Ruth Ruth, little girl from my youth—
now she's a stand-in for Otherness.
Otherness is death, death is Otherness.
Will you come back to me the way the dead sometimes
come back to the living, as if they were born again?
Does the arrow celebrate its return to the bow, and what about
the ball that returns from the wall to the hands of the child at play?

Oh, names without people, people without names,
all those secondhand names. I sometimes think about
the difference between borrowing a book and borrowing money.
In the one case, you must return the same thing.
In the other, you just give back

something of equal value,
like small change.

II

All those names, cleansed and purified, recycled
in the cycle, in the big mixer of names,
the name for its own sake and the name taken in vain,
names from over there and names
for over there, names of silence,
names of welter and waste.

Ruth Ruth, who died in my youth, now the two giants,
Yitgadal and Yitkadash, Magnified and Sanctified,
will watch over your death
in place of the two other giants, May He Bless and May He Keep,
who failed to watch over your life.
Ruth Ruth, thy hallowed name
magnified and sanctified,
His hallowed name, thy name.

12

Oh, the names of God, Blessed be His Name,
the Speakable Name and the Unspeakable Name.
Oh, family names for the dominion of day
and first names for the dominion of night,
names whispered in the dark.

In a piazza in Rome, I once saw a woman waiting
at a corner. I don't know how long
she stood there, or whether the one who hadn't come
did come in the end, or not. But after her death, God
will gently pry open her head, as He always does,
to look for the name of the one she truly loved.
And it won't be His name, it won't be His.

Jerusalem, Jerusalem, Why Jerusalem?

I

Jerusalem is forever changing her ways, like King David
who put on a crazy face to escape from death. The dead pretend
to be resurrected, the living to be dead,
peace puts on a scary mask of war, and war
changes its ways to peace. And we who dwell within her
are displayed in the shop windows of history with a wardrobe
of peculiar fashions and frozen gestures,
a heavenly expression on our faces for pilgrims and tourists
and the exalted angels. But what we really wanted
was to go wild in dark storerooms with an untrammeled joy
as in the Garden of Eden: "They were naked and were not ashamed."
And the saints who ascended on high in the distant past
and the astronauts who will ascend from Jerusalem in the distant
    future—
it's as if they are running away from her to heaven.
For compared to Jerusalem, even the outer space of infinity
is safe and protected, like a true home.

2

A city that has a wall, as Jerusalem has,
is like children who have a father,
and neither wall nor father can protect them any longer.
We cannot be fooled. I have seen people standing in a crowded bus
with weary extinguished eyes in their flaming faces
or flaming eyes in their weary extinguished faces.
And those who are standing raise their arms to hold on
as if rising in silent prayer, and they read the ads,
the writing on the wall above the bus windows: No Smoking,
Buy, Buy, Emergency Exit, just Buy, Buy!
Yes, we can be fooled.

3

Jerusalem sits in mourning, she's sitting shiva,
and those who come to visit and comfort
give her no peace, day or night. In their solicitude
they don't mention the name of the dead or the dead one's life,
they chat with her about world affairs and the daily grind.
With all the comings and goings, she has no time to mourn,
still unaware it is she who is both the mourned
and the mourner. They will not let her sit alone
so she keeps watch over the old houses of worship
the way a mother keeps the room of her son who died in the war
and will not change a thing in it. Will not even open the curtain.

4

The trees in Jerusalem try really hard to rustle like the sea,
and so do those who pray from their depths, and the lovers in their beds,
but we cannot be fooled.
Yes, we can be fooled.

5

Jerusalem is like an Atlantis that sank into the sea:
everything there is submerged and sunken.
This is not the heavenly Jerusalem, but the one down below,
way down below. And from the sea floor, they dredge up ruined walls
and fragments of faiths, like rust-covered vessels from sunken
prophecy ships. That's not rust, it's blood that has never dried.
And clay jars covered with seaweed, the corals of time and the fury
     of time
and coins from days gone by, the negotiable currency of the past.
But some very young memories are down there too:
a love-memory from last night, see-through memories
quick as glamor fish caught in a net, thrashing and splashing.
Come, let's throw them back into Jerusalem!

6

Jerusalem is a merry-go-round-and-round
from the Old City through all the neighborhoods and back to the Old.
And you can't get off. Whoever jumps off puts his life on the line
and whoever gets off at the final round has to pay again
to get back on for the rounds that have no end.
And instead of elephants and painted horses to ride,
there are religions that go up and down and turn on their axis
to the music of oily tunes from the houses of prayer.
Jerusalem is a seesaw: sometimes I dip down
into past generations, sometimes I rise up to the skies and then
I shriek like a child, feet swinging on high:
I want down, Daddy, I want down,
Daddy, get me down.
And that's how the saints all ascend to heaven,
like a child screaming, Daddy, I want to stay up here,
Daddy, don't get me down, Our Father Our King,
leave us up here, Our Father Our King!

7

In Jerusalem, everything is a symbol. Even two lovers there
become a symbol like the lion, the golden dome, the gates of the city.
Sometimes they make love on too soft a symbolism
and sometimes the symbols are hard as a rock, sharp as nails.
That's why they make love on a mattress of six hundred thirteen springs,
like the number of precepts, the commandments of Shalt and Shalt Not,
oh yes, do that, darling, no, not that—all for love
and its pleasures. They speak with bells in their voices
and with the wailing call of the muezzin, and at their bedside, empty shoes
as at the entrance of a mosque. And on the doorpost of their house
    it says,
"Ye shall love each other with all your hearts and with all your souls."

8

Why, of all places, Jerusalem? Why not New York
with her buildings on high and burrows down below
and tunnels and lower depths from which to call out:
O Lord, out of the depths have I cried unto thee.
Why Jerusalem, why me,
why not Athens, Egypt, Mexico,
India, Burma—the temples are already there,
the domes gilded, the pillars in place.

9

And there are days here when everything is sails and more sails,
even though there's no sea in Jerusalem, not even a river.
Everything is sails: the flags, the prayer shawls, the black coats,
the monks' robes, the kaftans and kaffiyehs,
young women's dresses and headdresses,
Torah mantles and prayer rugs, feelings that swell in the wind
and hopes that set them sailing in other directions.
Even my father's hands, spread out in blessing,
my mother's broad face and Ruth's faraway death
are sails, all of them sails in the splendid regatta
on the two seas of Jerusalem:
the sea of memory and the sea of forgetting.

10

Why, of all places, Jerusalem? Why not Babylon
with her Tower of Babel and her babbling tongues,
why not Petersburg with the mystery
of her white nights, white as priestly robes,
and her name changes: St. Peter, St. Lenin.
Why not Rome with her catacombs,
why not Mecca with her Black Stone,
why not Vancouver with her salmon

that ascend to her from the sea, crawling
on their bellies up the hard mountain slope
like atoning pilgrims, kosher pilgrims of fin and scale
that arrive at the blue heights, spawn, and die.

11

Shirts and dresses hung up to dry—right away you know
it's a holiday. White panties and undershirts mean peace and quiet.
But when flags are flying, you never can tell if it's a sign of peace
or of war, if they are left over from a festival
or a memorial for the dead. War and peace look the same
from a distance, as galaxies of new-formed stars look like
old stars that imploded and died.
We can be fooled. No, we cannot be fooled.
What summons us to prayer? The wail
of the fire engine, the police car, the ambulance.
And when prayers ascend on high, they fall
back down like shrapnel from anti-aircraft shells
that have missed their target. Then once again, a siren
summons us to prayer.

12

"How doth the city sit solitary," the prophet lamented over Jerusalem.
If Jerusalem is a woman, does she know desire?
When she cries out, is it from pleasure
or pain? What is the secret of her appeal?
When does she open her gates willingly and when is it rape?
All her lovers abandon her, leaving her
with the wages of love—necklaces, earrings,
towers and houses of prayer
in the English, Italian, Russian, Greek, Arab styles,
wood and stone, turrets and gables, wrought-iron gates,
rings of gold and silver, riots of color. They all give her

something to remember them by, then abandon her.
I would have liked to talk to her again, but I lost her
among the dancers. Dance is total abandon.
Jerusalem sees only the skies above her
and whoever sees only the skies above—
not the face of her lover—truly does lie solitary,
sit solitary, stand solitary, and dance all alone.

13

And there are days here when everything is gut, full gut or empty gut,
gut that ends up as violin strings or as sausage casing, the gut
of Jeremiah griping about the writhing in his gut,
a blind gut or a gut with vision that prophesies,
gut of history and gut of hysteria, the gut that links nothing
to nothing—no mouth, no way out, no body,
nothing but gut. All is gut.
All is vanity, all inanity, all is pain.

14

Why, of all places, Jerusalem? Why not London
with its gardens and palaces and towers and the chiming
from the top of Big Ben. Big Ben, a big old boy,
Big God, great God in the mists of holiness.

15

There are days here when all is mouth: fish mouth, mouth
of slaughtered lamb, blabbermouth, the mouth of a well,
of cantor and choir, pretty mouth, mouth of keyhole,
asshole, gaping mouth of the abyss,
mouth pious or profane, double-edged mouth, the mouth
of the ass that spake unto Balaam, the mouth of a camel baring its teeth.
And my mouth shall proclaim Thy glory.

16

In Jerusalem, hope springs eternal. Hope is like a faithful dog.
Sometimes she runs ahead of me to check the future, to sniff it out,
and then I call her: Hope, Hope, come here, and she
comes to me. I pet her, she eats out of my hand.
And sometimes she stays behind, near some other hope,
maybe to sniff out whatever was. Then I call her my Despair,
I call out to her: Hey, my little Despair, come here,
and she comes and snuggles up, and again
I call her Hope.

17

Two lovers talking to each other in Jerusalem
with the excitement of tour guides, pointing,
touching, explaining: These are my father's eyes you see
in my face, these are the sleek thighs I inherited from a distant mother
in the Middle Ages, this is my voice which traveled
all the way here from three thousand years ago,
this is the color of my eyes, the mosaic of my spirit,
the archaeological layers of my soul. We are holy places.
In ancient caves we can hide and write secret scrolls
and lie together in the dark.
Once in Ein Kerem in an abandoned cave I saw
rooster feathers and the torn dress of a woman
and I was filled with fury, my wrath was almost biblical.
In the courtyard of the orphanage, in the convent beside that cave,
there was suddenly a wild commotion and a rushing about
of young girls and nuns, a crazy she-goat, barking dogs.
Then stillness and a worn brown wall.

18

Sometimes Jerusalem is a city of knives.
Even the hopes for peace are sharp, to cut through

the hard reality. After a while, they grow blunt or brittle.
Church bells keep trying to ring out a calm round tone
but they grow heavy, like a pestle in a mortar pounding
artillery shells—muffled, leaden, trampling sounds.
The cantor and the muezzin want to sweeten their tune
but in the end, a piercing wail cuts through the din:
The Lord God of us all, the Lord is
one, one, one.

   19

I always have to go in the opposite direction to whatever
is passing and past. That's how I know I live in Jerusalem:
I go against the tide of pilgrims parading in the Old City,
brush by them, rub up against them, feel the weave of their clothes,
breathe in their smell, hear their talk and their song
as they fly past my cheeks like beautiful clouds.
Sometimes I get tangled in a funeral procession
and emerge at the other end, heading toward the good life.
And sometimes I'm held captive by the joy-parades and I raise my arm
like a swimmer against the stream, or as if to say: Go in peace,
go, go away, and I head for the other side, toward
my griefs and my peace. I go against the longings and the prayers
to feel their warm breath on my face,
the buzz and rustle of the stuff of longing and prayer.
This could be the start of a new religion,
like striking a match to make fire, like the friction
that sparks electricity.

   20

There are days when everyone says, I was there,
I'm ready to testify, I stood a few feet from the acccident,
from the bomb, from the crucifixion, I almost got hit, almost
   got crucified.

I saw the faces of bride and groom under the wedding canopy and almost
rejoiced. When David lay with Bathsheba I was the voyeur,
I happened to be there on the roof fixing the pipes, taking down a flag.
With my own eyes I saw the Chanukah miracle in the Temple,
I saw General Allenby entering Jaffa Gate,
I saw God.
And then there are days when everything is an alibi: wasn't there,
    didn't hear,
heard the explosion only from a distance and ran away, saw smoke but
was reading a newspaper, was staying in some other place.
I didn't see God, I've got witnesses.
And the God of Jerusalem is the eternal alibi God,
wasn't there didn't see didn't hear
was in some other place. Was some Place, some Other.

21

Why Jerusalem? Why not the sublime San Francisco?
After all, she already bears the name of that bird-loving saint,
and she has a golden gate, ascents and descents and ascents,
and a rumbling in the depths always ready to burst forth in fire
and pillars of smoke, as when God gave the Torah on Mount Sinai,
and an earth that opens its mouth wide, as in the Bible.

22

Why Jerusalem, why not Paris with her squares
and boulevards, arches of glory for the King of Glory,
her broad bridges over the narrow world.

23

There are days in this city when no one is himself
but somebody else's son. And they are called *Ibn, Ben,
Son, Sohn.* He is not he and you are not you
and I am not I but the son of I, Ibn Ezra and Ibn Musa,

Ben Abraham, Ibn Allah, Son of God.
And all of them gospeling what will be, even those
who cannot remember go around reminding the others,
and even Love laments the destruction of the Temple,
the rocking motions of the body in lament and in love are one.
And then there are days when everyone is somebody's father,
and they are all called *Abu*: Abu This, Abu That,
Father of Progeny, Father of Orphans, Father of Pains,
Father of Mercies, Abu-of-Us-All, Our Father Our King.

24

Longing for Jerusalem, for childhood in Jerusalem, in another
    faraway time:
the children of the Levites longing, now that they are old, in exile
by the waters of Babylon. They still remember singing
in the Temple when their voices had just begun to change.
At night they remind one another of their childhood:
Remember how we played hide-and-seek behind
the Holy of Holies, among the urns of frankincense,
near those drainage ditches around the altar, in the shadow
of the embroidered mantle on the Holy Ark,
between the cherubim?

25

Why Jerusalem, why me?
Why not another city, another person?
Once I stood at the Western Wall
when suddenly a flock of startled birds soared up,
shrieking and flapping their wings like bits of paper
with wishes scribbled on them, wishes
that flew out from between the massive stones
and ascended on high.

Conferences, Conferences:
Malignant Words, Benign Speech

I

Above the hotel gate, I saw a sign:
"International Conference on Inflammations of the Eye"
for those who have cried too much or not cried enough.
All of them with name tags on their lapels
like temporary nameplates in a cemetery or markers
in a botanical garden.
They approach one another as if sniffing, as if checking,
Who are you where are you from and when
was the last time you cried.
The subject of the morning session is "Sobbing:
The End of Crying or the Way It Begins." Sobbing
as soul-stuttering and griefstones. Sobbing
as a valve or a loop that links cry to cry,
a loop that unravels easily, like a hair ribbon,
and the crying—hair that fans out in profusion, glorious.
Or a loop that pulls into an impossible knot—
sobbing like an oath, a testimony, a cure.
Back in their cubicles, the women translators are busy
translating fate to fate, cry to cry. At night they come home,
scrub the words from their lips, and with sobs of happiness
they start loving, their eyes aflame with joy.

2

A conference on inflammations of the eye. Tears are always delegates
from a big salty sea, they never come from fresh water,
a flowing stream, a placid lake. And when was the last time
you cried? The translators sit and recycle it all to another
recycling plan that has no end, and the spirit of God
hovers above with the whirring wing-blades of a giant fan
whipping the air, the words whipped over and over like foam.
The closing session: "He cried like a dog.
The dog cried like a human being." That is the final meeting,

the undoing of all doctrines, the end of all conferences.
And above the door a sign, "Emergency Exit," lit by an eternal
red light. An eye inflammation of the cosmos
that has no cure.

   3

A conference on language: colloquial, baroquial, poetic, pathetic.
And the chance for a new language of war and peace:
Just as nouns and verbs in Hebrew change in the masculine and feminine
by adding a syllable or changing a vowel, making the sound longer
or shorter, so will it be with the language of war and, once again,
the language of war. And the final conference,
just me and myself: a panel of my body parts
addressing my soul, each with its set topic
and its allotted time—hands, feet, kidneys, heart,
intestines, reproductive organ, joy and pain.
And the close of the conference: reconvening inside to confer
with myself—no name tags, no translators, only words.
O my words, the good and the bad,
the changing and the changed. O my words—
the malignant words, the benign speech.

   4

Conferences and symposia, too numerous to count.
A conference on the import and export
of one religion to another, exporting Torah from Zion and babies
into the world, importing the dead. Or a major conference on Job:
dermatologists on skin diseases, anthropologists
on pain and suffering, legal scholars on justice and injustice,
God on the nature of Satan, and Satan on the notion of the divine.
Job's three friends, Bildad, Eliphaz, and Zophar, on the psychology
of suicide, the science of suicidology.
Zoologists on "The Leviathan: from Job to Paradise,"

and ceramicists on the type of potsherd Job used
to scratch himself. Scratching as a solution,
speech as a scratching in the throat or a scratching unto death,
till death do them part, the scratcher and the good potsherd.
And the translators translate pain to another kind of pain,
remembering to forgetting, forgetting to remembering,
curse to blessing and blessing to curse.
Sometimes they fall asleep in their cubicles like newborns
in their bassinets in the maternity ward.

5

A lecture on the soul. Live testimony. An animated lecture.
In the British Museum I saw a bird with the claws of a lion,
and a lion with a human head, and winged oxen.
I asked them: Why, what do you need that for,
isn't it enough that you are a lion, a bird, an ox?
And they answered: You soul-sotted creatures,
isn't it enough that you are human, of clay and humus made?
Why do you need these tacked-on souls
and a God that doesn't fit you, and emotions, besides?

6

The translators flee their burning cubicles,
run out into the streets, crying "Help!"
and make their way to other, calmer conferences.

7

A conference open to the public. The soul is formed before the body
like an infrastructure—a five-lane highway, straight and wide,
    tucked into
the landscape, so you can get from one place to another quickly, easily.
No: The soul is revealed only when the life of the body recedes,
like the narrow winding paths in the Judean Desert

that become visible only after many generations
of sheep and their barefoot shepherds.
A nocturnal conference: The soul is a search, the soul is a dance
of searches for whatever is lost. I frisk myself
and my clothes, patting softly then harder, looking for
an envelope, some ID, keys, small change, an important note.
I stand up, bend over, shake myself out,
reach my fingers deep into my pockets,
poke at my skin, my flesh.
People think I'm scratching myself. The soul is
an itch. Scratching reveals it, calms it down.

    8

Morning session: The body is a heavy stone that has dropped
into still waters. The soul is the ripple. The soul consists
of soft centrifugal rings that grow wider and wider.
A counter-session at noon: The body consists of waves
that ripple inward in centripetal circles,
smaller and smaller, closer and heavier,
to form the heavy soul at the bottom.

    9

The body is the workplace of the soul,
the body is the laboratory for experiments, inventions, innovations.

    10

The body wants to lock up the soul as if in a safe,
not to be opened until the will is read.
The will is the soul. The body is the safe,
the key is in God's hands. Or simply lost.

11

An afternoon session: "God and the Soul."
A Jew thanks God every day for restoring his soul.
But what would happen if one morning the body decided
it would like a different soul?

12

God in His mercy and thrift may decide to grant
a single soul to a number of human bodies.
Like a streetlight that illuminates several houses,
or a locomotive that pulls all the cars of a train?

13

Evening session: to lie on your belly in the dark,
bury your head in the pillow and, with your eyes closed,
to see stars more colorful, more lovely than those in the sky.

14

The translators, men and women, sit in their cells
and make honey, like bees, from all the buzz and babble:
a cultured honey behind their eyes,
a wild honey under their pubic hair.

My Son Was Drafted

I

My son was drafted. We brought him
to the station along with the other boys.
Now his face has joined the faces of those who say goodbye to me
from the passing windows of the buses and trains of my life,
faces in the streaming rain, faces
squinting in the sun. And now his face.
In the corner of the window, like a stamp on an envelope.

2

In a piazza in Rome near the Colosseum I wash my hands at a
    public faucet
and drink from my cupped palm, and meanwhile a red-haired woman
in a white dress who was sitting on a folding chair near a closed gate
is gone. When I lift my wet face
she is no more, flown away like a feather placed on the world
to check if the world is still breathing. The world
is still breathing, the world is alive,
the woman is still alive. We are alive, my son is still alive,
the white feather is still flying and living.
I want my son to be a soldier in the Italian army
with a crest of colorful feathers on his cap,
happily dashing around with no enemies, no camouflage.

3

I want to give him some advice: Listen, my son, don't change.
Remember: Thou art what thou art. On a hot day,
drink a lot of water—chug it down and change.
And another piece of advice I remember from my own wars:
When you go out for a night patrol, fill your canteen to the top
so the water won't make a sloshing sound and give you away.
That's how your soul ought to be in your body, large and full and silent.
(When you make love, make all the noise you want.)

And don't forget the window in your room that became
a window in the bus. At the end of all windows, there's a door.
The door giveth and the door taketh away.
And above all, don't forget the wisdom of the folding chair,
the joy of the colorful feathers,
the prophecy of the flying white feather.
And the vision of an old Italian city
where, at the end of tangled alleys, there's always
a piazza of sunlight and talk.

4

Birds know where to build their nests,
fish know where to spawn,
jasmine fills the air with its fragrance only at night,
a sea painted on a wall looks out
on the sea framed by a window.
(Have I ever mentioned that my father knew
the art of tying packages tight for transport?)
I want my son to be a soldier in the Vatican's Swiss Guard
with their coats of many colors, their sashes and blunt lances
glittering in the sun.

5

I would like to add two more commandments to the ten:
the Eleventh Commandment, "Thou shalt not change,"
and the Twelfth Commandment, "Thou shalt change. You will change."
My dead father added those for me.

6

My son was drafted. We visited him at the army base, in the desert,
the desolation that tents with their ropes and tent-pegs
try to make us forget. The whitewashed stones along the path
so blinding white-hot I covered my eyes

like a Jewish woman lighting the Sabbath candles.
I sat down on a stone near an empty can, and the music
of the wind in that empty can was all that had ever happened,
all that ever would. From the distant sand dunes I heard scattered shots
like a nervous, insistent thumbing through the Book of Life and Death.
My son's barefoot steps when he was a baby were louder
than his heavy boots in the fine mealy Negev sand.
I want my son to be a soldier in the British army,
guarding a palace in the rain. A tall fur hat on his head,
everyone staring at him while, without moving a muscle,
he is laughing inside.

   7

My children grew and flourished around tears and laughter
like fruit, like houses, but the tears and the laughter
stayed inside the kernel, just as they were. Our Father, Our King!
That's all for today on fathers and kings.
Go, my children whom I begot: Get yourselves into the next century,
where the tears and the laughter will continue, just as they were.
I remember giving them a stern warning:
"Never, never stick your hand out the window of a moving bus."
Once we were on a bus and my little girl piped up, "Daddy, that man
stuck his hand into the outside!"

That's the way to live: to stick your hand into the world's
infinite outside, turn the outside inside out,
the world into a room and God into a little soul
inside the infinite body.

   8

I taught them how to walk and now they are walking away from me.
I taught them how to speak to the world
and now they are teaching me to speak to my own heart.

I taught them to sleep, and taught myself to stay awake at night.
I am a camel with a hump of emotions, I'm a worrybear, the worries
are stored inside me in a layer of fat and hair. I'm a kangaroo
whose pouch emptied out. On my soul there's a place marked for pain
as on a form marked with a dotted line: "Cut here and return."
My head is a womb and my heart a garage and my hands
superfluous. Changes like that happen to me from time to time,
changing roles, changing places—change and exchange.
I am an expert on brittle yearnings
and blunted desires. If I were an angel, before I turned around
I would be too weary to fly with my wings.

9

My daughter looks more like my mother than like me or my wife.
Those daring magnificent leaps in the Genetic Games
that have no winners, or those sideways jumps
of the knight in chess—a phantom prophecy that snags us
with its hooks and lines into past and future.
Yes, my son was drafted. When he comes home for the night
he is silent, then he sleeps, and my daughter sleeps too.
There they are, sleeping in my house near the wall
of the Old City of Jerusalem, and I know
that a father is an illusion, just like that wall.
Neither one can protect. Can only love, and worry.

10

Children collect small hopes and the small change of charity
for cancer patients, heart patients, the blind
and God alone knows what else.
They come to the door and knock gently—like a heartbeat:
We've come...We've come...We've come....
Once I checked out the world with my children.
They were my Geiger counters, my depth gauges,

the thermometers and frigometers I used to seek, to check, to find.
Now they use me to probe the world that was and the world to come.

11

"The end of the matter: all has been heard." Now my daughter too
has been drafted. Now her face too is in the window
of the bus that slowly pulls out of the station. Now her face too
in the corner of the window like a stamp on an envelope.
    Like her brother.
Oh, those stamps, those letters sent off into the world,
those letters we send. Those names, addresses, numbers,
those colorful stamps, those faces.
And the thud of the censor's seal like the hammerblow of fate.

12

Now her face too, now she too,
and I want to give her some advice:
Don't forget the tremendous power of hair that fans out free and open,
and the tremendous power of hair pulled back, coiled tight
like a dancer's.

13

As for that piazza in Rome, the water goes on streaming from the faucet,
and the flags are out for a feast day,
and the song of the fife and drum is heard in the land;
as for the woman who vanished, and as for the feathers,
they go on vanishing and flying in the world of time.
And the illusion of walls in Rome and Jerusalem
goes on deluding, along with all the other questions and chimeras.
And as for my children and their journeys away from life,
may the two Kaddish giants Yitgadal and Yitkadash
protect them as they protected my father and mother—
my children in their lives, my parents in their deaths.

1

End of summer. After extreme torture by the last *hamsin*,
summer confesses its guilt and I say: The dry tree is regal, the thorn
glorious, the thistles that give themselves over to their hardness
are marvelous. The parasite ivy is more beautiful than the host,
and the dry tendrils of the vine cling to the bramble in love.
White feathers at the mouth of a cave tell of a brutal death
but also of the beauty of great wings beating.
The fissures and cracks in the tormented earth will be the map
of my life. From here on, bird-watchers will determine history,
geologists will plot out the future, meteorologists
will read the palm of God's hand, and botanists
will be experts in the tree of knowledge, good and evil.

2

With a squeeze of my fingers, like a lover's pinch, I check
if the figs are ripe. I will never know what counts as death
to figs, being left on the tree or rotting on the ground,
what their inferno is and their Eden, what their salvation
and what their resurrection. The mouth that eats them—
is it heaven's gate or the mouth of hell? Once upon a time,
trees were the gods of human beings. Now perhaps we
are gods to the trees and their fruit.
The turtledove calls out in love to its brothers the carob trees;
it knows nothing of the eons of evolution
that lie between them, it calls and calls and calls.

3

The upturned gaze to see if clouds—
what does it light upon along its way: walls, balconies,
the laundry of longings hung out to dry, wistful windows, rooftops,
sky. The open hand stretched out to see if raindrops—
that is the most innocent hand of all,

the most believing, more prayerful
than all the worshipers in all the houses of prayer.

4

In the airplane in the sky, those who are returning home
sit beside those who are leaving, and their faces are the same.
Atmospheric currents of longing form the rain that's about to fall.
In the Crusader ruins, the autumn squill blooms long after
its leaves come up in the spring, but it knows what happened
in the long dry summer between. Its brief eternity.
The water towers in Yad Mordechai and Negba were kept in ruins
as a remembrance. What an autumn nation we are,
to celebrate the fall of Masada and its suicides,
the ruin of Jotapata and Betar and the destruction of Jerusalem
at the Western Wall. Remnant of remnants. Like someone who keeps
shoes that are falling apart, a torn sock, tattered letters as remembrances.
All this only to postpone a little the hour of death.
And all our lives, everything that happens in them, that stirs and swarms
     inside them,
is a hedge around life. And death too is a hedge around life.

5

I want to sing a psalm of praise to all that remains
here with us and doesn't leave, doesn't wander off like migratory birds,
will not flee to the north or the south, will not sing "In the East
     is my heart,
and I dwell at the end of the West." I want to sing to the trees
that do not shed their leaves and that suffer
the searing summer heat and the cold of winter,
and to human beings who do not shed their memories
and who suffer more than those who shed everything.
But above all, I want to sing a psalm of praise

to the lovers who stay together for joy, for sorrow and for joy.
To make a home, to make babies, now and in other seasons.

6

I saw a tree in fall whose hardened seeds rattled and clacked
inside their pods. A man's seed streams and slithers out, sticky,
and is swallowed up without a sound.
Thus hath the seed of a tree preeminence
over the seed of a man:
it is like a cheerful toy rattle, and that is its love song.

7

For love must be spoken, not whispered, that it may be
seen and heard. It must be without camouflage,
conspicuous, noisy, like a raucous laugh.
It must be a kitschy commercial for "Be fruitful and multiply":
a perky amazing "Be fruitful" and a hard-edged, tortured "multiply"
of the human species—sweet frosting for a bitter life.
Love is words and flowers that attract insects and butterflies
in the field, but also the floral pattern on a woman's dress.
It's the delicate skin of the inner thigh, it's underwear
down to the bottoms of the soul and overwear up to the heavens,
it's public relations, the pull of earth dwellers to earth,
Newton's law of gravity
and the law of levity of the divine. Hallelujah.

And Who Will Remember
the Rememberers?

1

Verses for Memorial Day, a psalm of remembering
for the war dead. The generation of memory-veterans
is dying out. Half at a ripe old age, half at a rotten old age.
And who will remember the rememberers?

2

How does a monument come into being? A car goes up in a red blaze
at Sha'ar HaGay. A car burnt black. The skeleton of a car.
And next to it, the skeleton of some other car, charred in a
    traffic accident
on some other road. The skeletons are painted with anti-rust paint, red
like the red of that flame. Near one skeleton, a wreath of flowers,
now dry. From dry flowers you make a memorial wreath,
and from dry bones, a vision of resurrected bones.
And somewhere else, far away, hidden among the bushes,
a cracked marble plaque with names on it. An oleander branch,
like a shock of hair on a beloved face, hides most of them.
But once a year the branch is cut back and the names are read,
while up above, a flag at half-mast waves as cheerfully
as a flag at the top of the flagpole, light and easy,
happy with its colors and breezes.
And who will remember the rememberers?

3

What is the correct way to stand at a memorial ceremony?
Erect or stooped, pulled taut as a tent or in the slumped posture
of mourning, head bowed like the guilty or held high
in a collective protest against death,
eyes gaping frozen like the eyes of the dead
or shut tight, to see stars inside?
And what is the best time for remembering? At noon
when shadows are hidden beneath our feet, or at twilight

when shadows lengthen like longings
that have no beginning, no end, like God?

    4

And what should our lament be? David's lament over Saul and Jonathan:
"Swifter than eagles, stronger than lions," that is what our lament
    should be.

Had they really been swifter than eagles
they would have soared high above the war
and would not have been hurt. From down here, we would have
    seen them
and said: "There go the eagles! There is my son, my husband,
    my brother."

And had they really been stronger than lions
they would have stayed like lions, not died like human beings.
They would have eaten out of our hands,
we would have stroked their golden manes,
we would have tamed them in our homes, with love:
My son, my husband, my brother, my husband, my son.

    5

No one has ever heard of the fruit of the jasmine,
no poet has sung its praises,
they all sing drunken odes to the jasmine flower,
its heady scent, its color, white against dark leaves,
the vigor of its blossoming and the force of its short life—
a butterfly's life or the life of a star.
No one has ever heard of the fruit of the jasmine.
And who will remember the rememberers?

6

No one praises the blossoms of the vine, everyone praises
the fruit of the vine, and blesses the wine.
Have I mentioned that my father, in the wisdom of his hands,
knew how to prepare parcels for transport,
packed tight and sealed tight
so they wouldn't come undone along the way like me?
So much death in everything, so much packing and transport,
so much open that will never close again, so much closed
that will never open.

7

And who will remember? And what do you use to preserve memory?
How do you preserve anything in this world?
You preserve it with salt and with sugar, high heat and deep-freeze,
vacuum sealers, dehydrators, mummifiers.
But the best way to preserve memory is to conserve it inside forgetting
so not even a single act of remembering will seep in
and disturb memory's eternal rest.

8

Seeking roots in the Warsaw cemetery.
Here it is the roots that are seeking. They burst
from the ground, overturn gravestones,
and clasp the broken fragments in search
of names and dates, in search
of what was and will never be again.
The roots are seeking their trees that were burned to the ground.

9

Forgotten, remembered, forgotten.
Open, closed, open.

The Jewish Time Bomb

On my desk is a stone with "Amen" carved on it, one survivor fragment
of the thousands upon thousands of bits of broken tombstones
in Jewish graveyards. I know all these broken pieces
now fill the great Jewish time bomb
along with the other fragments and shrapnel, broken Tablets of the Law
broken altars broken crosses rusty crucifixion nails
broken houseware and holyware and broken bones
eyeglasses shoes prostheses false teeth
empty cans of lethal poison. All these broken pieces
fill the Jewish time bomb until the end of days.
And though I know about all this, and about the end of days,
the stone on my desk gives me peace.
It is the touchstone no one touches, more philosophical
than any philosopher's stone, broken stone from a broken tomb
more whole than any wholeness,
a stone of witness to what has always been
and what will always be, a stone of amen and love.
Amen, amen, and may it come to pass.

NOTES

I Wasn't One of the Six Million:
And What Is My Life Span? Open Closed Open

No. 4, page 6, line 1, **Open closed open**: cf. the rabbinic tale: "Unto what may the fetus in its mother's womb be likened? Unto a notebook that is folded up. Its hands rest on its temples, elbows on thighs, heels against buttocks, its head lies between its knees. Its mouth is closed and its navel open.... When it comes forth into the air of the world, what is closed opens and what is open closes." Babylonian Talmud, Tractate Niddah, chapter 3, folio 30a. A variant appears in Leviticus Rabbah 14:8.

I Foretell the Days of Yore

No. 7, page 13, line 5, **"In the East is my heart"**: from a well-known poem by Yehuda Halevi (c. 1075–1141), one of the leading poets of the Golden Age of Hebrew poetry in Spain. Halevi's poem became the epitome of Jewish longing for Zion through the ages. Our translation here adapts that of Emma Lazarus.

The Bible and You, the Bible and You, and Other Midrashim

No. 1, page 19, line 1, **How did Gideon choose his army?**: Judges 7:5–6.
    line 13, **the rolling barley cake**: Judges 7:13.
No. 2, page 19, line 3, **"This is the blessing"**: from Deuteronomy 33:1, the final portion in the annual cycle of Torah readings.

line 12, **Writings**: third division of the Hebrew Bible, after the five books of Moses and Prophets.

No. 14, page 25, line 3, **Ezekiel's vision of the chariot**: Ezekiel 1.

No. 17, page 26, line 1, **Balaam**: Canaanite priest who blessed Israel when ordered to curse it by Balak, King of Moab; cf. Numbers 22–24.

Once I Wrote Now and in Other Days: *Thus Glory Passes, Thus Pass the Psalms*

No. 1, page 31, line 1, *Now and in Other Days*: Amichai's first collection of poetry (1955).

No. 2, page 31, line 2, **the Huleh swamp**: Draining the Huleh swamp in the 1950s—both to provide arable land and to fight malaria—was considered one of the proudest achievements of the Zionist pioneers. This threw the fragile ecosystem of the area off balance, however, and the Huleh had to be flooded again recently.

line 12, page 32, **"All men are false"**: Psalm 116:11.

No. 3, page 32, line 2, **"This is the last battle"**: from "The Internationale," the international workers' anthem.

No. 7, page 33, line 1, **the Memorial Days**: In the Israeli calendar, Holocaust Memorial Day is followed by the Memorial Day for Fallen Soldiers.

lines 1–2, **the names of streets**: Streets in Israel are often named for important figures in the history of Zionism.

No. 8, page 34, line 6, **the battle of Huleikat**: crucial battle in the Negev, during the Israeli War of Independence, in which Amichai saw active combat.

No. 9, page 34, line 6, **the sons of Korah**: Levite singers in the Temple ritual, mentioned in the headings of a group of psalms.

No. 10, page 35, line 13, **"Lord, O Lord"**: Exodus 34:6; cf. Psalms 86:15.

Gods Change, Prayers Are Here to Stay

No. 1, page 39, line 9, **the town where I was born**: Würzburg, in Bavaria, Germany, where the Jewish community was attacked in 1147 at the time of the Second Crusade.

No. 2, page 40, lines 14–15, **"turns, turns," "whirling and turning"**: see Ecclesiastes 1:6, "The wind ... whirleth about continually, and the wind returneth again according to his circuits."

line 16, **"without a beginning, without an end"**: from *Adon Olam* ("Lord of the Universe"), a familiar synagogue hymn.

No. 4, page 40, line 7, **Song of Ascents** (Hebrew *Shir Ha-Ma'alot*, literally "The Song of the Stairs"): heading of Psalms 120–134, referring perhaps to the fifteen steps leading to the Temple, on which the Levites would pause to chant psalms.

No. 5, page 41, line 6, **"Seek ye the Lord"**: Isaiah 55:6.

No. 7, page 41, line 1, **"Our Father, Our King"** (Hebrew *Avinu Malkenu*): litany recited during the Ten Days of Penitence between Rosh Hashana and Yom Kippur, which concludes with the plea, "Our Father, Our King! Be gracious unto us and answer us, for we have no good works of our own. Deal with us in charity and lovingkindness, and save us."

No. 9, page 42, line 4, **Simchat Torah** (literally "Rejoicing with the Torah"): festival marking the completion of the annual cycle of Torah reading in the synagogue.

No. 13, page 42, line 1, **spice boxes**: ceremonial objects, often of filigreed silver, filled with aromatic spices, passed around during the Havdalah service to mark the end of the Sabbath and welcome the new week.

No. 13, page 43, line 8, **long metal hands** (Hebrew *yad*, "hand"): ritual pointers, usually of silver, used when reading from the Torah scroll in the synagogue.

line 11, **Seder plates**: platters displaying symbolic foods in the Passover ritual meal, during which the story of the exodus from Egypt is retold.

line 12, **kiddush**: blessing recited over wine on the eve of the Sabbath or a festival.

No. 16, page 44, line 1, **tallis** (here in the familiar Ashkenazi spelling): fringed shawl with stripes of blue or black, traditionally worn by Jewish men at prayer.

No. 17, page 45, lines 1, 7, 10, **kosher; chewing their cud; cleft**: The dietary laws of *kashrut* (ritual purity) determine, among other things, what kind of animals may or may not be eaten; meat is kosher only if it comes from animals that chew their cud and have cleft hoofs. See Leviticus 11, Deuteronomy 14.

No. 21, page 46, line 2, **the women's section:** In an Orthodox synagogue, the women are segregated from the men by a partition (Hebrew *mechitsah*).

line 8, **"Blessed be He who has made me according to His will":** part of the morning prayers recited by Orthodox women. Men are required to say, "Blessed be He who has not made me a woman."

No. 22, page 47, line 2, **"Come, O Sabbath bride":** traditional hymn in which the Sabbath is personified as bride and queen. **Friday nights:** Like all Jewish holy days, the Sabbath begins at sunset on the previous evening.

line 6, **Kaddish:** prayer for the dead, traditionally recited by the surviving male members of the deceased's family.

David, King of Israel, Is Alive: Thou Art the Man

No. 1, page 51, line 2, **"alive forever":** from "David, King of Israel, Is Alive Forever," a popular Israeli folk song and dance.

No. 3, page 52, line 10, **tower, etc.:** Tower of David, Citadel of David, City of David, King David Street, King David Hotel—principal sites on the tourist circuit in Jerusalem.

line 13, **Nahal David:** riverbed in the desert near the Dead Sea.

No. 4, page 52, line 5, **"Thou art permitted unto me now":** an adaptation of the rabbinical divorce decree, "Thou art hereby permitted to any man."

line 7, **Rabbah:** Rabbat-Ammon, i.e., Rabbah of the Ammonites, site of modern Amman; cf. 2 Samuel 12:26.

No. 6, page 53, line 10, **the poor man's ewe lamb:** 2 Samuel 12:3.

My Parents' Lodging Place

No. 1, page 57, line 2, [Moses] **Ibn Ezra** (c. 1055–1135): one of the leading poets of the Golden Age of Hebrew poetry in Spain. The phrase "lodging place" in Ibn Ezra's poem "My Thoughts Awoke Me" alludes to Jeremiah's yearned-for refuge, a "lodging place in the wilderness" (Jeremiah 9:2).

No. 4, page 58, line 5, **"remember"** and **"keep":** from *Lekha Dodi,* a hymn welcoming the Sabbath; cf. Exodus 20:8 and Deuteronomy 5:12.

What Has Always Been
No. 1, page 63, line 1, **The poet Rachel**: Rachel Blovstein (1890–1931), a modernist poet born in Russia, one of the first women poets who wrote in Hebrew in pre-statehood Israel; many of her poems have been set to music and are part of Israeli popular culture.

line 4, **what has been . . . the sun**: cf. Ecclesiastes 1:9.

line 13, **moshav**: a type of community in Israel consisting of individual leaseholds farmed cooperatively.

No. 5, page 64, line 1, **Gath and Galon**: kibbutzim in southwestern Israel.

No. 9, page 66, line 1, **Nineteen forty-eight**: Israel declared its independence on May 14, 1948.

Israeli Travel: Otherness Is All, Otherness Is Love
No. 1, page 69, line 8, **orchard**: The Hebrew *pardes* ("orchard") is an acronym for four exegetical approaches to the sacred texts. The rabbis warned against the dangers of mystical exegesis: in the Talmudic parable of "Four Who Entered the Orchard" (Tractate Hagigah 14b), only one, Rabbi Akiva, emerged intact; the one called *Acher* (literally "Other") became a heretic.

No. 2, page 69, line 1, **Ein HaShofet**: kibbutz in northern Israel, named for U.S. Supreme Court Justice Louis Brandeis.

No. 11, page 73, line 1, **Yad Mordechai**: kibbutz founded by a group of refugees from Poland in 1943; site of a memorial to the uprising in the Warsaw ghetto, and to one of its leaders, Mordechai Anielewicz. A bloody battle in the 1948 War of Independence is reenacted here in a Sound-and-Light show.

Evening Promenade on Valley of the Ghosts Street
No. 1, page 77, line 1, **Valley of the Ghosts Street** (Hebrew *Emek Rephaim*): fashionable street in the German Colony (Hebrew *Moshava Germanit*) section of Jerusalem.

No. 2, page 77, line 5, **Rabbi Gershom** (c. 960–1028): rabbinic authority of early Ashkenazi Jewry. Although best known for his ban on polygamy, Rabbi Gershom also forbade opening mail directed to others.

Houses (Plural); Love (Singular)

No. 1, page 89, line 4, **Ein Gedi**: oasis near the Dead Sea where David took refuge from King Saul (1 Samuel 24). Ein Gedi is associated with love poetry; see Song of Songs 1:14. A kibbutz and a national park are now found on this site.

line 5, **Rejeh, Sideir**: two tributaries of Nahal David, near Ein Gedi.

line 8, **mezuzah**: encased parchment scroll, inscribed with the verses Deuteronomy 6:4–9 and 11:13–21, affixed to the doorposts in Jewish homes. It contains the injunction "And thou shalt love the Lord thy God with all thine heart, and with all thy soul, and with all thy might" (Deuteronomy 6:5).

The Language of Love and Tea with Roasted Almonds

No. 1, page 93, line 1, *Layla*: The word *layla* "night" appears to be feminine in form, but is construed as masculine. Hebrew marks all nouns, animate and inanimate, for gender.

line 6, *Elohim*: The common biblical word for God is plural in form, though it is normally construed in the singular.

No. 2, page 93, line 9, **prayer of Closing the Gates** (Hebrew *Ne'ilah*, "locking up," i.e., the Heavenly Gates): concluding service of the Day of Atonement.

No. 11, page 97, lines 1–2, **story of David and Jonathan**: cf. 1 Samuel 20.

The Precision of Pain and the Blurriness of Joy: The Touch of Longing Is Everywhere

No. 1, page 101, line 3, **shiva**: the seven days of mourning following the death of a close relative.

No. 2, page 101, line 8, **Shekhinah**: God's indwelling presence, i.e., the divine immanence in Creation, or its manifestation in the people of Israel. In Kabbalah, the feminine aspect of God.

In My Life, on My Life

No. 12, page 112, line 1, **may I rest in peace** (Hebrew *alay ha-shalom*, literally "Upon me, peace"): a play on *alav ha-shalom*, "May he rest in peace," traditionally said after mentioning the name of a deceased person.

No. 13, page 113, line 1, **Chevra Kadisha** (literally "The Sacred Fellow-ship"): a group that fulfills the sacred duty of purifying and preparing a dead body for burial. According to Orthodox practice, men's bodies are prepared by men, and women's bodies by women.

line 14, **God Full of Mercy** (Hebrew *El Maleh Rachamim*): from the funeral prayer, "Grant perfect rest beneath the wings of Thy Divine Presence."

line 15, **Womb** (Hebrew *rechem*) has the same root letters as "mercy" (Hebrew *rachamim*).

Jewish Travel: Change Is God and Death Is His Prophet
No. 1, page 117, line 1, **"I will lift up mine eyes"**: Psalm 121:1.

lines 6, 8, **"Who shall ascend the mountain of the Lord?...[He that hath] clean hands and a pure heart"**: Psalm 24:3–4.

line 10, **"Out of the depths"**: Psalm 130:1.

lines 11, 12, **"green pastures," "still waters"**: Psalm 23:2.

line 15, **"Valley of the Shadow of Death"**: Psalm 23:4.
No. 2, page 118, line 14, *Makom* ("Place"): one of the designations of God.
No. 6, page 120, line 6, **Palmach**: commando units of the Haganah (the pre-state underground army), which played a major role in the 1948 Israeli War of Independence.
No. 7, page 120, line 4, *ketubah*: illuminated scroll in Aramaic that serves as the marriage contract.

line 6, **"The voice of the bridegroom"**: part of the traditional bless-ings in a Jewish wedding ceremony; cf. Jeremiah 7:34.

line 12, **"what of the night?"**: Isaiah 21:11.
No. 9, page 121, line 5, **"the dead praise not the Lord"**: Psalm 115:17.

page 122, line 11, *kohen* ("priest"): descendants of a priestly family that traces its origins to Aaron, the first priest. According to tradition, the priestly blessing is performed with the fingers separated and outstretched in a characteristic gesture of benediction.
No. 10, page 122, line 3, *mikveh* (or *mikveh tahara*, literally "a pool of purifi-cation"): ritual bath used primarily by Orthodox women to purify them-selves after birth and menstruation.
No. 13, page 124, line 12, **minyan**: quorum of ten or more Jewish males over thirteen years of age, required for any prayer service.

Names, Names, in Other Days and in Our Time

No. 1, page 127, line 1, **Yehúda:** colloquial Hebrew pronunciation of the proper name Judah; the formal pronunciation is Yehudá, also the name for Judea. *Yehudi,* from the same root, means "Jew" or "Jewish." In everyday speech, names are usually pronounced according to the penultimate stress-pattern of Ashkenazi (European) Hebrew; in the formal language, names are stressed on the final syllable, as are most words in modern Israeli Hebrew.

No. 4, page 128, line 9, *Hoshana* ("Please save!"): prayer recited on Hoshana Rabba, the seventh day of Sukkot, considered a minor Yom Kippur; a plea for absolution from the sins of the past year and for a merciful judgment from God in the year to come.

No. 5, page 129, line 20, *Shema Yisrael* ("Hear, O Israel"): the basic credo of Judaism, proclaiming the absolute unity of God (cf. Deuteronomy 6:4–9); daily prayer, and final prayer of the dying, affirming the oneness of God.

No. 7, page 130, line 1, **Paul Celan** (1920–1970): the great Jewish poet, born in Czernovitz, Rumania. His parents were deported and shot in 1941; Celan himself was incarcerated in a German forced labor camp. After the war he settled in Paris, where he continued to write in German. Celan drowned himself in the Seine.

No. 8, page 130, line 13, **dispensation:** from the Kol Nidre prayer on the eve of Yom Kippur: "Our vows shall not be vows, our bonds shall not be bonds, and our oaths shall not be oaths." Ancient formula for absolution from vows rashly made to God.

No. 10, page 131, line 1, **Ruth:** Amichai's childhood love who perished in the death camps; recurs as a character throughout his poetry and prose.

No. 11, page 132, line 8, **Yitgadal and Yitkadash:** the opening words of the Mourner's Kaddish, "Magnified and Sanctified [be His great name in the world which He hath created according to His will]."

line 10, **May He Bless and May He Keep:** from the Priestly Blessing: "The Lord bless thee and keep thee; the Lord make His face to shine upon thee and be gracious unto thee; the Lord turn His face unto thee and give thee peace."

Jerusalem, Jerusalem, Why Jerusalem?

No. 1, page 135, lines 1–2, **King David...put on a crazy face:** 1 Samuel 21:12–15.

No. 13, page 140, line 3, **the writhing in his gut**: Jeremiah 4:19.

No. 15, page 140, lines 5–6, **the mouth of the ass that spake unto Balaam**: Numbers 22:28.

No. 17, page 141, line 9, **secret scrolls** (Hebrew *ha-megilot ha-gnuzot*): the Dead Sea Scrolls, discovered in the Qumran caves of the Essene sect in the Judean desert.

No. 20, page 143, line 7, **Chanukah miracle in the Temple**: During the Maccabean revolt against Antiochus Epiphanes, a cruse of oil which should have lasted only one day sufficed to light the Temple for eight days.

No. 21, page 143, line 6, **an earth that opens its mouth wide**: "And the earth opened her mouth, and swallowed them up together with Korah" (Numbers 26:10).

Conferences, Conferences: Malignant Words, Benign Speech

No. 11, page 151, line 1, **"The end of the matter"**: concluding verses of the Book of Ecclesiastes.

Autumn, Love, Commercials

No. 1, page 163, line 1, *hamsin*: hot desert wind that blows in Israel at the beginning and the end of summer.

No. 4, page 164, lines 9–10, **Masada** (fell A.D. 73); **Jotapata** (fell A.D. 66): sites of the first rebellion against Roman occupation. **Betar** (fell A.D. 135), ended the Bar Kochba Rebellion of 132–135 against Rome.

No. 6, page 165, line 4, **preeminence**: "A man hath no preeminence above a beast: for all is vanity" (Ecclesiastes 3:19).

And Who Will Remember the Rememberers?

No. 2, page 169, line 2, **Sha'ar HaGay**: memorial on the road to Jerusalem consisting of the skeletons of armored vehicles that line the sides of the highway; commemorates the Jewish convoys that fell in their effort to relieve the siege of the city in the War of Independence.

No. 4, page 170, line 1, **David's lament**: 2 Samuel 1:17–27.

ACKNOWLEDGMENTS

We are very grateful to Yehuda Amichai for entrusting us with *Open Closed Open*, the fruit of nearly a decade's work on his part. During the entire process of translation, Yehuda and Hana Amichai collaborated by telephone and fax; we deeply appreciate their critical comments and their unfailing encouragement.

A Translation Fellowship from the National Endowment for the Arts and a Marie Syrkin Fellowship from the Jerusalem Foundation provided support and validation.

Leon Wieseltier championed this project from the outset and, to our delight, offered to read the finished manuscript. We benefited from his inestimable literary and editorial skills, his devotion to the Hebrew text, and his profound knowledge of the Jewish sources.

We are particularly indebted to Amichai Kronfeld, whose critical acumen and sensitivity to the nuances of the Hebrew left their imprint on every page of this book. His exacting criticism set a standard that we worked overtime to meet. We could not have accomplished our task without his invaluable contribution.

We are fortunate to count among our friends a number of fine poets and translators who helped us with unstinting generosity. Anita Barrows read the manuscript at an early stage, giving us the benefit of her keen sensitivity to rhythm and phrasing. Tess Gallagher, with her great poetic intuition, reached straight to the heart of the Hebrew, offering ingenious solutions to intractable problems. Gail Holst-Warhaft brought her deep understanding of Amichai's work to bear in detailed critiques of early and late versions of the manuscript. Stanley Moss's insightful comments enabled us to revise and polish the final draft. We also wish to thank Robert Alter, Benjamin Bloch, and Carol Cosman for their sensitive suggestions. A heartfelt thank you to Eliyah Arnon, who assisted us with research on geographical and historical references and helped in untold other ways.

We were very happy to work with Drenka Willen, our editor at Harcourt, whose gracious ways and meticulous attention to detail are unusual in today's world of publishing and Joan Benham, copy editor extraordinaire. Our agent Georges Borchardt and his assistant DeAnna Heindel helped, as always, with their wise counsel and valiant support.

Chana Bloch wishes to thank Mills College for a course release which provided the gift of time, and the artists' colony Yaddo for the gift of place—a creative haven in which to work.

Our gratitude to the editors of the following journals, where earlier versions of poems in this collection first appeared: *American Poetry Review, The Atlantic Monthly, Forward, Grand Street, Hungry Mind Review, Inquiring Mind, Judaism, Lilith, Living Text, Marlboro Review, Modern Poetry in Translation, Moment, The Nation, The New Republic, The New Yorker, The New York Review of Books, Parnassus, Partisan Review, Poetry, Poetry Flash, Reform Judaism, Salmagundi, The Threepenny Review, Tikkun, The Times Literary Supplement* (London), *Tin House, World Literature Today,* and *The Yale Review.*

Most of all, we would like to thank each other. Our search for the *mot juste* often sent us with queries to unlikely places, including the Army surplus store, the maternity ward at Alta Bates Hospital, the Chevra Kadisha, and Fat Apple's bakery. Sustained by the richness of Amichai's work and the all-too-rare pleasures of collaboration, we were each other's best teachers.